C000000314

Crossway Bible Guide

Series editors: Ian Coffey (NT), Stephen Gaukroger (OT)
New Testament editor: Steve Motyer

Titles in this series

Romans:
Crossway Bible Guide

David Coffey

Crossway Books Leicester

CROSSWAY BOOKS
38 De Montfort Street, Leicester LE1 7GP, England

First published 2000

British Library Cataloguing in Publication Data
A catalogue record for this book is available from the British Library.

ISBN 1–85684–200–2

Set in Palatino

Typeset in Great Britain

Printed in Great Britain by Omnia Books Ltd, Glasgow

CONTENTS

Seven routes through Romans

3. The basis for evangelism (11 studies)

4. Practical Christianity (5 studies)

5. The faith factor (5 studies)

6. Christians and Jews (7 studies)

7. Paul the friend (6 studies)

Welcome!

These days, meeting together to study the Bible in groups appears to be a booming leisure-time activity in many parts of the world. In the United kingdom alone, it is estimated that over one million people each week meet in home Bible-study groups.

This series has been designed to help such groups and, in particular, those who lead them. These Bible Guides are also very suitable for individual study, and may help hard-pressed preachers, teachers and students too (see 'How to use this Bible Guide').

We have therefore enlisted authors who are in the business of teaching the Bible to others and are doing it well. They have kept in their sights two clear aims:

1. To explain and apply the message of the Bible in non-technical language.
2. To encourage discussion, prayer and action on what the Bible teaches.

All of us engaged in the project believe that the Bible is the Word of God – given to us in order that people might discover him and his purposes for our lives. We believe that the sixty-six books which go to make up the Bible, although written by different people, in different places, at different times, through different circumstances, have a single unifying theme: that theme is Salvation. This means free forgiveness and the removal of all our guilt, it means the gift of eternal life, and it means the wholeness of purpose and joy which God has designed us to experience here and now, all of this being made possible through the Lord Jesus Christ.

How to use this Bible Guide

These guides have been prepared both for personal study and for the leaders and members of small groups. More information about group study follows on the next few pages.

You can use this book very profitably as a personal study guide. The short studies are ideal for daily reading: the first of the questions provided is usually aimed to help you with personal reflection (see 'How to tackle personal Bible study'). If you prefer to settle down to a longer period of study, you can use groups of three to five studies, and thus get a better overview of a longer Bible passage. In either case, using the Bible Guide will help you to be disciplined about regular study, a habit that countless Christians have found greatly beneficial. (See also 'Seven routes through Romans' for methods of selecting studies if you do not intend to use them all.)

Yet a third use for these Bible Guides is as a quarry for ideas for the busy Bible teacher, providing outlines and application for those giving talks or sermons or teaching children. You will need more than this book can offer, of course, but the way the Bible text is broken down, comments offered and questions raised may well suggest directions to follow.

How to tackle personal Bible study

We have already suggested that you might use this book as a personal study guide. Now for some more detail.

One of the best methods of Bible study is to read the text through carefully several times, possibly using different versions or translations. Having reflected on the material, it is a good discipline to write down your own thoughts before doing anything else. At this stage it can be useful to consult another background book. See 'Resources' on page 14 and 'For further reading' on page 235. If you are using this book as your main study resource, then read through the relevant sections carefully, turning up the Bible references that are mentioned. The questions at the end of each chapter are specifically designed to help you to apply the passage to your own situation. You may find it helpful to write your answers to the questions in your notes.

It is a good habit to conclude with prayer, bringing before God the things you have learned.

If this kind of in-depth study is too demanding for you and you have only a short time at your disposal, read the Bible passage, read the comments in the Bible Guide, think round one of the questions and commit what you have learned to God in a brief prayer. This would take about fifteen minutes without rushing it.

How to tackle your group Bible study

1. Getting help

If you are new to leading groups, you will obviously want to get all the help you can from ministers and experienced friends. Books are also extremely helpful and we strongly recommend a book prepared by the editors of this series of Bible Guides: *Housegroups: The Leaders' Survival Guide* edited by Ian Coffey and Stephen Gaukroger (Crossway Books, 1996). This book looks at the whole range of different types of group, asking what is the point of it all, what makes a good leader, how to tackle your meeting, how to help the members, how to study, pray, share and worship, and plenty of other pointers, tips and guidelines.

This book is a 'must' for all leaders of small groups. It is written by a team of people widely experienced in this area. It is available at your local Christian bookshop. If you have difficulty in obtaining a copy, write to Crossway Books, Norton Street, Nottingham NG7 3HR, UK.

2. Planning a programme with your Bible Guide

This guide is a commentary on God's Word, written to help group members to get the most out of their studies. Although it is never ideal to chop up Scripture into small pieces, which its authors never intended, huge chunks are indigestible and we have tried to provide a diet of bite-sized mouthfuls.

If you want to get an overview of the Bible book in a series of meetings, you will need to select appropriate studies for each meeting. Read them yourself first and prepare a short summary of the studies you are tackling for your group. Ideally you could write it on a sheet of A5 paper and hand a copy to each member.

Do not attempt to pack more than one study into one meeting, but choose the crucial one, the study which best crystallizes the message.

If you do not intend to cover the whole Bible book, choose a series of studies to suit the number of meetings you have available. It is a good idea to use consecutive studies, not to dodge about. You will then build up a detailed picture of one section of Scripture. Alternatively, there are seven suggested routes through Romans on pp. 8–10.

3. Resources

You will find any or all of these books of great value in providing background to your Bible knowledge. Put some of them on your Christmas list and build up your library.

New Bible Dictionary or *New Concise Bible Dictionary* (IVP)
New Bible Atlas (IVP)
New Bible Commentary (21st Century edition) (IVP)
Handbook of Life in Bible Times, John Thompson (IVP)
The Bible User's Manual (IVP)
The Lion Handbook to the Bible (Lion Publishing)
The Message of the Bible (Lion Publishing)
NIV Study Bible (Hodder & Stoughton)
The Bible with Pleasure, Steve Motyer (Crossway Books)

The relevant volume in the IVP Tyndale Commentary series will give you reliable and detailed help with any knotty points you may encounter.

4. Preparing to lead

Reading, discussing with friends, studying, praying, reflecting on life ... preparation can be endless. But do not be daunted by that. If you wait to become the perfect leader you will never start at all. The really vital elements in preparation are:

▶ prayer (not only in words but an attitude of dependence on God: 'Lord, I can't manage this on my own')

▶ familiarity with the study passage (careful reading of the text, the Bible Guide study and any other resource books that throw light on it) and

▶ a clear idea of where you hope to get in the meeting (notes on your introduction, perhaps, recap what was covered at the last meeting, and what direction you hope the questions will take you in – don't force the group to give your answers).

Here is a short checklist for the busy group leader:

Have I prayed about the meeting?
Have I decided exactly what I want to achieve through the meeting?
Have I prepared the material?
Am I clear about the questions that will encourage positive group discussion?
Am I gently encouraging silent members?
Am I, again gently, quietening the chatterers?
Am I willing to admit ignorance?
Am I willing to listen to what the group members say and to value their contributions?
Am I ready not to be dogmatic, not imposing my ideas on the group?

Have I planned how to involve the members in
discovering for themselves?

Have I developed several 'prayer points' that will help
focus the group?

Are we applying Scripture to our experience of real life or
only using it as a peg to hang our opinions on?

Are we finding resources for action and change or just
having a nice talk?

Are we all enjoying the experience together?

What can we expect to learn from Romans?

God's rescue plan for the world
The gospel in a nutshell
Why Jesus died and rose from the dead
The Christian life from A to Z
The basis for evangelism
The work of the Holy Spirit
God's plan and purpose for Jews and non-Jews
How to live with diversity in the local church
How to turn a vision for mission into an action plan

Finding your way around this book

In our Bible Guides we have developed special symbols to make things easier to follow. Every study therefore has an opening section which is the passage in a nutshell.

The main section is the one that *makes sense of the passage*.

Questions

Every passage also has special questions for personal and group study after the main section. Some questions are addressed to us as individuals, some speak to us as members of our church or home group, while others concern us as members of God's people worldwide. The questions are deliberately designed:

▶ to get people thinking about the passage

▶ to apply the text to 'real life' situations

▶ to encourage reflection, discussion and action!

As a group leader you may well discover additional questions that will have special relevance to your group, so look out for these and note them in your preparation time.

Stop and look

This feature gives us the chance to stand back from the action and take stock. It gives a summary of what to look for in the passages we are about to read, and useful background material.

Digging deeper

Some passages require an extra amount of explanation, and we have put these sections into two categories. The first kind gives additional background material that helps us to understand something factual. For example, if we dig deeper into the Gospels, it helps us to know who the Pharisees were, so that we can see more easily why they related to Jesus in the way they did. These technical sections are marked with a spade.

Stop and think

The second kind of background section appears with passages which highlight important themes or teaching. Bible references and questions will help you think them through. Write down your answers or use them as a framework for group discussion.

Unfolding Romans

The letter you are about to study has been exceptionally important in the story of the Christian church. In most centuries the thinking of Christian leaders and their friends has been shaped in profound ways by the teaching of Paul's letter to the Romans.

Romans is not an easy read. But, as with most difficult challenges in life, constant discipline will be repaid with rich rewards. One person has described a study of Romans as a spiritual blood transfusion for the local church.

As you read through Romans, it will help if you keep in mind:

▶ some basic background information;

▶ the purpose behind the writing of this letter; and

▶ an idea of its structure.

Background: what's the postmark?

Paul probably wrote this letter from the province of Achaia in Greece, in a three-month period during AD 55–57. It is thought that Acts 20:2–3 refers to the time when the letter was composed. Enjoying the hospitality of a Christian called Gaius, Paul also had the assistance of a secretary called Tertius, whom we read about in 16:22–23. Tertius probably wrote the epistle in longhand as Paul dictated his thoughts. Paul is staying in Achaia on his way to Jerusalem. While in Macedonia and Achaia he had collected a famine offering and wished to deliver this gift of money personally to the church in Jerusalem.

He is writing to the Christians in Rome, not an individual church but rather a number of congregations scattered across the city. (See 'The house congregations in Rome', page 224). Paul would be aware that a letter to the imperial capital would quickly go into circulation throughout the Mediterranean world of Christian congregations.

Purpose: just writing because ...

Paul had concluded his pioneering missionary work at the eastern end of the Mediterranean. (You can read about this major part of his ministry in Acts, starting at chapter 13.) Now Paul is seeking to establish personal links with the congregations in Rome (look at Romans 1:8–15 and 15:14–33 together).

Paul has never visited Rome and has not met most members of the congregations based in the capital city of the empire, so he has to do two things in this letter. First, he has to introduce himself and present his spiritual CV as a servant of Christ Jesus. Unhelpful stories may have been circulating about this controversial preacher, who, until his dramatic conversion, worked hard to arrest Christians who were witnessing for Jesus Christ (Acts 9:1–2). For this reason he takes longer than usual in the introduction to his letter (1:1–7).

Secondly, he wants to present a comprehensive overview of the Christian gospel. Paul has been preaching and teaching the gospel for about twenty years in a broad range of contexts. His understanding has deepened and matured through the years, and, with a break of three months to hand, he has decided to present in one letter a concise outline of the gospel of Christ Jesus.

In the formative years of the first-century church, this concise account was exactly what local congregations needed to help them interpret the Old Testament story. It would also serve as a companion to the Gospel records of the life and ministry of Jesus, which were already in circulation. So Romans was written to strengthen the faith and knowledge of believers and to equip them in the task of explaining the gospel to those outside the church.

Thirdly, Paul has long-term plans for a pioneering mission work in Spain, and believes the congregations in Rome could have a major part to play in this mission project. His vision is illustrated in the map on p. 22.

Structure: what does he have to say?

After some preliminary introductions (1:1–15), Paul outlines the main themes he will unfold throughout the letter and presents the gospel of God in a nutshell (1:16–17). He then moves on through four main sections of sustained teaching:

▶ The gospel of God we require (1:18 – 3:20)

▶ The gospel of God we are given (3:21 – 8:39)

▶ The gospel of God that was refused (9 – 11)

▶ The gospel of God worked out in daily living (12 – 15)

Paul concludes his letter with a section of greetings and farewells (16:1–27).

PS

I express my gratitude to the three churches I have pastored at Whetstone, Leicester; North Cheam, Surrey; and Upton Vale, Torquay, whose members gave me every encouragement, as a pastor, to study the Bible in order to share its insights with others. I know the influence this letter has had on my pastoral and evangelistic ministry. I have seen the minds of Christians opening up to the practical benefits which come from a deeper understanding of this important book of the New Testament. I now encourage you, with a humble dependence on the Holy Spirit, to make a journey through Romans.

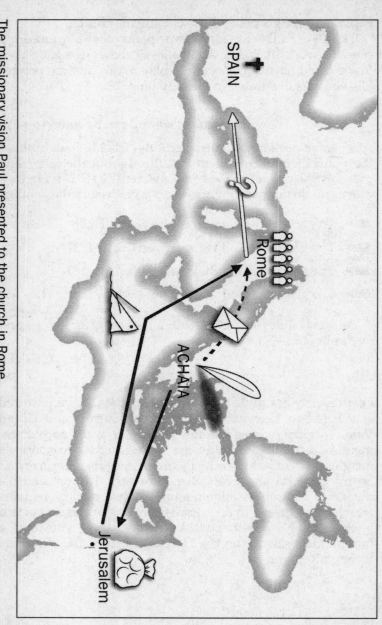

The missionary vision Paul presented to the church in Rome

SPAIN

Rome

ACHAIA

Jerusalem

THE GOOD NEWS

Romans 1:1–17

Romans 1:1

Called by God

Paul sets out his credentials as a Christian leader and reminds his readers that to be called by God carries spiritual obligations.

When you send a letter to someone you normally begin by writing your address and the date and then 'Dear So-and-so'. In the first century you would start by writing your own name, the name of the person receiving the letter, and then a personal greeting.

This is the style Paul adopts in chapter 1, except that his greeting is longer than usual (verses 1–7). This is because, never having visited Rome, he wants to impress two things on his readers. First, he is an authentic Christian leader appointed by God. Secondly, he holds an orthodox understanding of the gospel. Passages such as 2 Corinthians 11 and Acts 21:20–21 suggest that rumours circulated about Paul's authority to minister and the 'strange' views he was teaching, and Paul may feel that such false reports need correcting.

Paul's life was dramatically changed when he met the risen Lord on the road to Damascus (Acts 9). God transformed the bitter persecutor of Christ and his people into an enthusiastic missionary of Christ and his gospel. To emphasize that this transformation was not due to his own cleverness or natural ability, and to explain the nature of his ministry, he applies three terms to himself. He is a servant of Christ Jesus; called to be an apostle; and set apart for the gospel of God.

A servant of Christ Jesus

Although most English versions use the term 'servant', Paul actually uses the word for 'slave'. In Roman times a slave was the total possession of someone else. The word 'slave' conveys most vividly that Paul sees himself as completely devoted to Jesus Christ and always at his service. He is thinking not of the cruel and humiliating aspects of slavery but of his exclusive allegiance to Jesus Christ, and of Christ's right to rule his life. God determines what Paul will do, and as an obedient slave he stands in the tradition of other servants of God such as Moses (Joshua 14:7) and Joshua (Joshua 24:29). When we read that Paul has been prevented from visiting Rome (1:13), we need to see in this phrase the Christian servant following the instructions of his Lord for his diary of ministry engagements. This is more than human frustrations surrounding travel plans.

Called to be an apostle

The title 'apostle' was used by Jesus for the twelve disciples he called (Luke 6:13). The word means 'someone who is sent as a messenger'. Paul states that he was a proud and arrogant man before his conversion (Philippians 3:4–11), but once the Lord had met him on the Damascus road he had a radically different view of himself. He knows one can't appoint oneself to be a messenger from God, which is why he uses the word 'called'.

He is deeply conscious that God had a special calling for him from his birth (Galatians 1:15), and this calling was confirmed to him by the man who led him to Christ (Acts 9:15). This knowledge of his calling to be an apostle did not fill him with feelings of superiority. In fact, he felt the reverse. Paul felt inadequate to be an apostle and it was only the grace of God working in him that enabled him to use the title (1 Corinthians 15:9–10).

Set apart for the gospel of God

Because Paul has a deep conviction that God has sent him into the world to perform a specific task, he is able to say he has been set apart for the gospel. As a former Jewish rabbi, he knows that the name 'Pharisee' means 'separated one', and Paul had led a life of separation. This new experience of being separated does more than make him a preacher of the gospel. He makes plain in chapters 12 – 16 that gospel people are distinguished by a gospel lifestyle (12:1). Paul has been called to live and preach the gospel.

God's calling carries spiritual obligations

It is significant that Paul links his own calling and the calling of the believers in Rome (verses 5–7). He applies his understanding of his own calling to the church in Rome and its evangelistic ministry: like himself, the Christians in Rome are called to belong to Jesus Christ (verse 6) and called to be saints (verse 7), and both Paul and they have received this calling in order to call other people to become followers of Jesus Christ (verse 5).

From the beginning of the letter there is an emphasis on the life-changing work of God in people, and Paul himself is the best example of a changed life. It is amazing to think that someone who felt he was doing God's work in persecuting the earliest members of the Christian church (remember he was present when Stephen was stoned to death, Acts 8:1) can now describe himself as a servant of Christ Jesus. And it is no small miracle that there are Christians in Rome. This was the capital of the Roman empire, the seat of government for the most powerful ruler in the known world. It was a centre for high culture and sophisticated sinning. There were certainly easier places to plant churches. And yet here in Rome, the miracle that changes people into followers of Jesus Christ had taken place. They are loved by God and called to be saints (verse 7). The spiritual obligation of being saved in order to serve is a theme that Paul will develop as the letter proceeds.

Questions

1. If you were writing to someone who did not know you, how would you introduce yourself and briefly convey the most important things in your life?
2. How do the fellowship, worship and ministry of your local church equip members for a life of obedience to God in the world? If they don't, how can you change things to achieve that goal?
3. What are the special problems and difficulties of being Christians in a big city? Is it the same in all cities? Are there opportunities to match the difficulties? Are you grasping them?

Romans 1:1–7

The message that caused trouble all over the world

Paul briefly describes the gospel, emphasizing that it comes from God himself. He reminds us that we are saved in order to serve.

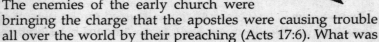

Paul has just told us that the special function of an apostle, central to his calling, was to communicate the gospel. The enemies of the early church were bringing the charge that the apostles were causing trouble all over the world by their preaching (Acts 17:6). What was so revolutionary about this message? Paul provides a threefold analysis: the gospel's source, character and content.

The gospel's source

Paul describes the Christian message as 'the gospel of God' (verse 1). The word 'gospel' would be familiar to the citizens of Rome. It means 'good report'. They would use 'gospel' to refer to the worship of the Roman emperor. Reports of his coming of age, his accession to the throne, or the birth of a royal child would be referred to as 'good news'.

Paul says this 'gospel' is the good news that originates with God. It is God's gospel. He is its source, and it originates in his concern to rescue people from their sin. The word is used in other parts of the New Testament in the same way (see Mark 1:14; 2 Corinthians 11:7; 1 Peter 4:17).

The gospel's character

This gospel of God was not a novelty. It had not been invented by the early apostles. It did not begin when Jesus commenced his ministry. This gospel of God fulfilled all that had been promised through the Old Testament prophets (verse 2), and this is what made it trustworthy (see Acts 2:14; 17:2; 1 Peter 1:10). Jesus bore witness to this in own ministry, making it clear that these promises were pointing to him (John 5:39–40; Luke 24:25–26).

We need greater confidence in the authority of Scripture, remembering the truth of the unity of the Old and New Testaments in the saying: 'The New is in the Old concealed; the Old is in the New revealed.' It was vitally important to the early church that the gospel fulfilled the Old Testament.

The gospel's content

The good news we communicate is centred on the person of Jesus Christ. We do not merely make known his *teachings*.

He is central *as a person* to the gospel. It has been said that Jesus came not to preach a gospel, but in order that there might be a gospel to preach. This explains why Paul spells out clearly who Jesus is. He is a human Saviour (verse 3), a divine Saviour and a Spirit-filled Saviour (verse 4).

▶ He is a human Saviour with an earthly family tree. He is the very Messiah who was promised to his ancestor David centuries before (2 Samuel 7:11–14).

▶ He is a divine Saviour, who through his earthly ministry was revealed as the Son of God in humility and suffering (Hebrews 5:7–10), and by his resurrection is declared with power and exaltation to be the Son of God (Romans 1:4).

▶ He is a Spirit-filled Saviour. The Bible says that Jesus was conceived by the Holy Spirit (Luke 1:35), and all his ministry was conducted in the power of the Holy Spirit (Luke 4:1). By the power of the same Spirit he was raised from the grave.

The good news we are called to communicate to our world doesn't consist of helpful ideas people might like to try out. It's about the Christ who died and is risen, and who one day will come again to earth. He has sent *us* the same Holy Spirit who empowered his ministry. As the exalted Lord, he has poured out upon his church the power of the Holy Spirit, who comes to work out in our lives all that Jesus Christ has accomplished for us. This Holy Spirit imparts clarity, conviction and courage as we take up the challenge of being messengers of the gospel to our generation.

Saved to serve

We sometimes use this phrase, 'saved to serve', to describe the nature of the Christian life, and this is what rules Paul's understanding of the gospel.

He is aware that his salvation and his calling to be an apostle have placed him in the position of an undeserving person who has received an unexpected gift. But he is also aware that such grace-gifts from God carry a spiritual responsibility. They can never be used for personal enjoyment (see also 1 Corinthians 15:10; 1 Timothy 1:12–14).

God had saved Paul in order to give him an evangelistic ministry, calling people to faith in Jesus Christ. Paul reminds the Christians in Rome that they too have a similar privilege: to be witnesses to the gospel (verse 5).

Questions

1. List examples of Bible promises which you have seen fulfilled and which have confirmed your faith in the gospel. Why is it important to understand the unity of the Old and New Testaments?
2. 'Christianity is all about trying to love your neighbour.' How does Paul's description of the gospel's content differ from this popular view?
3. Do you think that spreading the good news is a job just for specially called and gifted people like Paul (verse 5)? Or should we all do it? The Romans were 'called to be holy' (verse 7); does this include spreading the good news? What else might it mean?

The relationship between the Testaments

The Old Testament is often called the 'cradle of the gospel'. The New Testament is filled with references to the Old Testament, many of them prefaced by the words 'As it is written' (e.g. Romans 3:10; 8:36; 14:11). The best examples in Romans are the use of the Genesis passages on Abraham (4:1–25) and on Adam (5:12–21).

Paul and the early Christians based their writings on the Old Testament because they found Christ there. The divine plan had been progressively unfolded from the opening pages of Genesis, and had come to a climax in Jesus Christ, whose coming fulfilled the Old Testament Scriptures (Romans 1:2). This is essential to Paul's thinking. Jesus himself bore witness to this truth.

▶ He believed that his life on earth fulfilled Scripture, and began his preaching ministry by quoting Isaiah 61:1–2 (Luke 4:18–21).

▶ His teaching is based on the authority of the Old Testament (e.g. Matthew 12:3–5; 19:4–6).

▶ The Old Testament Scriptures are meant to lead us to Jesus (John 5:39, 45-47).

Read the story of the two disciples on the road to Emmaus (Luke 24:1–32). Which Old Testament scriptures did Jesus use to teach the two disciples the good news of the gospel?

Romans 1:8–15

Unfulfilled ambitions

Paul explains why he wants to visit the Christians in Rome.

Only twice in Romans does Paul express himself in personal terms: here in verses 8–15 and later in 15:14–33. We get an interesting insight into Paul's relationship with the Roman Christians if we read the latter passage straight after 1:15. Look again at the introduction, 'Unfolding Romans', for some suggestions why Paul wrote to this church in Rome. In these verses he explains why he was so eager to visit this group of Christians.

He appreciates them

It is likely that Paul is dictating this letter, for his secretary Tertius gets a mention at the end (16:22). Like any good secretary, Tertius would know the feeling when the boss begins a sentence of dictation with 'First', and then gets so caught up in the excitement of a long paragraph that he forgets the 'Secondly' and 'Thirdly'. But Paul has reason to get carried away with enthusiasm. After all, there is a vibrant Christian community in Rome, and its reputation is worldwide (verse 8).

Rome was the capital city everyone wanted to visit at least once in a lifetime. This was the city whose government had brought peace to the world and was the centre of a civilization that has left its mark on the world even of our own time. Rome was a recognized cultural capital for poets and artists. It was also a mecca for worldly lifestyles and the practice of all manner of sin and evil-doing. It was said concerning some of the inhabitants of Rome that they drank iniquity like water. Humanly speaking, not unlike some modern-day cities, it was impossible to imagine Christians existing in such a hostile atmosphere.

No wonder Paul says with pardonable exaggeration, 'Thank God there are Christians in Rome!' It meant a lot to struggling churches in other parts of the world to know that the church of Jesus Christ had been firmly planted in the capital city of the empire under which they lived.

He prays for them

Here we see two aspects to the ministry of Paul: he is the travelling preacher (verse 9) and the praying pastor (verse 10). Every time he prays for the Christians in Rome he asks the Lord to make it possible for him to visit them. For someone who had never visited the city, Paul reveals an amazing knowledge of the church membership (see chapter 16). It is likely that he has gained this information through his close tent-making friends, Aquila and Priscilla (Acts 18:1–3).

We can sometimes be quite casual when we tell people we are praying for them, but Paul is in earnest when he says he is praying for these people, and he calls on God as a witness to this serious commitment to prayer partnership. Notice how he calls on God in prayer elsewhere in his writings (1 Corinthians 1:23; Galatians 1:20; Philippians 1:8). What a wonderful inspiration Paul provides on how to offer prayer support for global mission!

With our modern communication systems, we can maintain contact with what is happening in the church of Jesus Christ worldwide, wherever we are situated, by developing prayer partnerships with specific churches.

He longs to encourage them

Paul longs to visit the church in Rome, and yet his motivation at all times is to do the will of God. This inward pull is clear in verse 10, as if Paul were saying, 'The longer the wait, the greater the ache.'

He has planned on many occasions to visit them (verse 13). Contrary to some rumours which may be circulating, he is not frightened of preaching in a large capital city, nor is he uninterested in what has been happening in this strategic centre of witness.

Most of us have to cope with the tension between pleasing ourselves and doing the Lord's will, and these two are not always compatible. Paul has been following the directions of the Lord, and he knows exactly what will happen when God does open the door for the visit. He and the Roman Christians will encourage one another through the exercise of spiritual gifts and ministries (verses 11–12). Paul has a realistic estimate of the gifts that God has given both to him and to the believers in Rome (see 12:3–7) and he is looking for mutual encouragement, which he describes as a potential harvest (verse 13). He may also be hoping to see some healing of the broken relationships in the church (which he tackles in chapters 14 and 15).

He has an obligation towards them

Paul is not saying that he has an obligation to visit Rome because they have been on his list of cities to visit and his arrival is now long overdue. The obligation to his friends in Rome is founded in his obligation to Jesus Christ. It is his obligation to the Christ who died and rose again for him that gives rise to his obligation to all those others for whom Christ died and rose again. As Jesus demonstrated in his own ministry, the good news of the gospel is for sharing with needy people (Mark 2:17).

If we have received the benefits of the gospel, we must not hoard it selfishly. We have an obligation to share the good news with people from diverse backgrounds. Verse 14 reflects a central theme of Romans: broadening the membership of God's family to include non-Jewish people from all nations, cultures and people groups. In today's language we might equate 'Greeks' and 'non-Greeks' with cultured and uncultured people, and the 'wise' and 'foolish' with educated and less educated people. Paul comes from an orthodox Jewish background and yet has a very broad missionary vision. God has called him to engage in evangelism among people totally different from himself. He encourages a racially and culturally diverse church to see the evangelistic potential of Christian unity (see Romans 15:7). His missionary vision that Rome might become a centre of outreach to Spain will become clearer in 15:24. We should ask ourselves whether we possess the same conviction and eagerness to share the gospel with all kinds of people (verse 15). If we are called to engage in cross-cultural mission, do we realize the importance of offering to the world a Christian community which is culturally diverse, multi-ethnic and yet united in Christ?

Questions

1. Can you identify any groups of people in your neighbourhood who are being neglected by your church?

What can you do about this?

2. Paul saw Rome as a strategic centre for the spread of the gospel. What are the strategic places in your community that could make a big impact if the gospel took root there? Does this strategy fit with your answer to question 1?

3. Share in your group what you know about the church in each continent of the world. How can you discover more?

4. How do you think Paul, as a missionary strategist, would use the means of communication available today?

Romans 1:16

The gospel in a nutshell (1)

Paul introduces some great themes of the letter to the Romans.

In the opening bars of a symphony, the main musical ideas are briefly introduced before they are explored in more detail in the four movements. The leading thoughts that Paul will unfold in his letter of sixteen chapters are introduced here in a nutshell of two verses (16–17).

Someone has found that the word 'God' occurs 153 times in Romans, an average of once every forty-three words. This is more than any other single theme. The importance of this statistic is that God is the author of the gospel that is good news for all people, Jewish and Gentile.

A gospel with dignity and power

Paul's statement that he is not ashamed implies that believers are sometimes tempted to be ashamed of the very gospel that has saved them. Jesus recognized the possibility that his followers would be ashamed of him and his teaching (Mark 8:38). The early church experienced ridicule when they proclaimed the resurrection of Jesus (Acts 17:32). Paul knows from his experience in writing to another church that people can be ashamed of the followers that Jesus gathers around him (1 Corinthians 1:26–29). In the capital city of the world, it was a daunting task to claim that an unknown carpenter from Nazareth was the Saviour of the world and the hope of all humankind.

And the shame remains today. There will always be intellectual, social and moral shame to overcome when presenting the gospel. It is in the nature of the gospel that the cross will look like nonsense and will be a stumbling-block in the eyes of human wisdom (1 Corinthians 1:20–25).

The secret we need to remember is that the gospel is not a good idea but God's power at work to save. The Roman nation had reason to be proud of their power structures. Their military power could subdue nations. Their naval power ruled the waves. Their cultural power gave the world great literature, law and art. Their technical power constructed roads that radiated from Rome throughout the known world. Rome's city sewer system was a credit to the power of first-century technology.

But Paul knew that this advanced and cultured nation was powerless when it came to changing people's lives. By contrast, the gospel of God has such a dynamic when it is preached that it releases an immeasurable power among the hearers (Acts 2:36–37). It is more than advice for helpless people; the Holy Spirit leads people to understand the seriousness of what the gospel is saying (John 16:8–11).

Because the gospel expresses God's power and not worldly power, there are strange dimensions to its dynamic. You can be simultaneously weak and strong (2 Corinthians 12:9); poor and rich (2 Corinthians 8:9); dead and living

37

(Galatians 2:19–20); and rejected by the world as a person of no significance yet accepted by God as someone of great value (1 Corinthians 1:18–31).

A gospel with a purpose and a constituency

The purpose of this powerful gospel is *salvation*. 'Salvation' means all the blessings that God alone can provide in answer to human need.

The various aspects of salvation will be explained as the letter proceeds. We shall discover that it includes deliverance from guilt, complete recovery from the disease of sin and release from its tyranny. Salvation is a past achievement (Ephesians 2:5) as well as a present process (2 Corinthians 2:15) and an anticipated future event (Romans 13:11). It also has cosmic dimensions (Romans 8:18–27).

The gospel is intended for everyone who believes. Regardless of race, nationality, social class or education, it is explicitly for every human being.

In stating that it is first for Jewish people, then for Gentiles, Paul is only following the order in which God chose to speak to people in human history regarding his plan of salvation. Salvation began with the Jewish people because they were first chosen by God and, in the Old Testament days, were, spiritually speaking, a highly privileged nation. This is why Psalm 80:17 describes Israel as God's right-hand man. Jesus sent his disciples first to the lost sheep of the house of Israel (Matthew 10:5–6). Whenever possible, Paul and the early missionaries went first to the Jewish quarter of any community they visited.

The Jews may have been first in line for the gospel, but since the life, death and resurrection of Jesus the good news is now open to all people, whatever their background. Jesus made this clear in his own ministry by opening the door to include non-Jewish people (John 3:16; 4:27). The fact that God has designed his gospel for every kind of person is not a new element in the plan of salvation; it was included in the ancient promise to Abraham (Genesis 12:3). This is why we shall read more about this Old Testament character when we come to chapter 4.

But the word 'everyone' is qualified by the phrase 'who believes'. Each person who hears the gospel must respond to it personally and make it his or her own.

This is the power of the gospel in action, making it effective in the lives of people from every conceivable background. By the power of the gospel they come to believe the good news about Jesus Christ.

Questions

1. In which parts of your life (e.g. work, home, college, sports club) are you most tempted to keep quiet about your commitment to Christ? What would help you to say with Paul, 'I am not ashamed of the gospel'?
2. In your group, share stories of the way the power of God has changed people. Or think about what he has done in your own life. How do these stories increase your confidence in presenting the gospel to others?
3. God is able to save Jews and Gentiles (verse 16). How do you answer the charge that religions, especially Christianity, *divide* groups, races and nations rather than unite them? (Think of Northern Ireland, the Balkans, Indonesia, Nigeria, Israel ...)

Romans 1:17

The gospel in a nutshell (2)

Human intellect alone cannot understand the gospel. We need a special revelation from God, to which we must respond in faith.

How can we come to know God personally? What if we lead a good life and try to keep the Ten Commandments: does this alone make us  acceptable to God? What happens to those Jewish people who expect a promised Messiah but refuse to believe that Jesus is the Saviour of the world? Verse 17 reminds us that we cannot work out answers to these questions with our minds alone; they have to be revealed to us by God.

What the gospel reveals

In the gospel God reveals who he is, what he has done and what he gives us.

- ▶ The gospel reveals *who God is*. His loving actions are in keeping with his righteous character. As Judge of all the earth (Genesis 18:25), he always delivers just judgments.

- ▶ The gospel reveals *what God has done*. He is a righteous God who keeps his promises and comes to our rescue in Jesus Christ.

- ▶ The gospel reveals *what God gives us*. Through Jesus' sacrifice on the cross, he puts us right with himself and grants us a righteous status.

▶ However good we may be, God saves us by a righteousness that comes from beyond ourselves. It puts us in the clear with God and totally changes the way we live.

Questions

1. If you had never heard of the Bible, how would you expect people to united with God? By meditation? Good deeds? Good luck? Religious rituals? How else? How does verse 17 cut across these ideas?
2. Imagine that you have to present an assembly at your local school to a group of thirteen- and fourteen-year-old children. How would you explain 'faith' to them?
3. Habakkuk 2:4 (the verse Paul quotes) was God's response to Habakkuk's agonized question over the suffering of his people Israel at the hands of the Babylonians: why do you think Paul alludes to this? What does facing suffering have to do with faith?

Righteousness

'Righteousness' is an important word in Romans (where it is used thirty-three times), and we need to understand it well. We think of righteousness as a *moral virtue*, something people can attain. But Paul's use of the word reflects his Jewish background. To him, righteousness was first and foremost a *legal standing*. A 'righteous' person was acquitted of all charges, and was in right standing before the law.

In the Bible, 'the righteousness of God' refers to *who he is* (he is a righteous God: Genesis 18:25; Psalm 45:6); to *what he does* (he comes to our rescue: Isaiah 45:21; 46:13); and to *what he achieves* (he places us in right standing before himself: Romans 5:17; 2 Corinthians 5:21).

It is this third meaning that is to the fore in Romans. Righteousness is the right standing with God that he achieved for us through the sacrifice of Jesus on the cross. We receive it by trusting Jesus Christ alone, and are acquitted of our sins by faith in him (see especially 1:17; 3:5, 21–22, 25–26; 5:17.

THE BAD NEWS

Romans 1:18 – 4:25

The gospel reveals God's way of making people right (1:16–17). But we can't be made right until we know we are in the wrong and are willing to be put right. What happens when we don't know or aren't willing? So long as we feel confident in our own understanding of how we can enjoy right relations with God, we will never turn to Christ. We need a true diagnosis of the human condition, and this is what Paul gives us in these remaining verses of chapter 1. Paul is like a courtroom lawyer as he presents the case against four groups of people and finds each group equally guilty under God's law.

It will prove helpful to identify these four groups before proceeding to examine them individually in more detail:

▶ the godless pagans, who are idolatrous in their thinking and immoral and antisocial in their behaviour (1:18–32);

▶ the upright moralizers, who criticize the downward trends of the society of their day and readily associate with Paul's trenchant criticisms of the godless pagans, but who fail to observe in their own lifestyles the high ethical standards they demand of others (2:1–16);

▶ the outwardly religious, the spiritually privileged Jewish people who are proud of their traditions but fail to keep the very law they boast about (2:17 – 3:8);

▶ the whole human race, underlining that no human being will escape God's judgment; everyone is guilty before God (3:9–20, 23).

Romans 1:18–23

Godless thinking

Paul describes human nature at its worst. God's just judgment is against all humankind. There is no excuse for idolatry, for God's reality is clear for everyone to see.

A contrasting revelation

Paul sets out a revelation of God as both saviour (verse 17) and judge (verse 18). When we respond in faith to God's way of putting us in the right, we have the privilege of knowing him as our saviour, friend and Lord. But the gospel also reveals God as judge. His judgment comes when we refuse to let God be God in his own world. Love and wrath are not incompatible, as we often think. Because God is love, he cannot remain passive in the face of sin. He sets his face against evil. He personally opposes sin, and the cross of Jesus Christ is where we see the full measure of both his love and his wrath.

God's wrath

When human beings do not acknowledge God as the creator of the world and go their own way, does this mean God has been shut out of his own world? Is he helpless to act within his world? Has he abandoned the world he created and left it to unravel in its own disorder? No! What kind of God would let evil flourish in this world as if it didn't matter? God does not leave sinners to their own way of living. He does something to oppose sin. This is his wrath in action. That is why saying 'yes' to God brings good consequences. When we say 'no' to God we suffer a different set of consequences. We experience God's wrath.

We may object to the idea of God's wrath on the ground that anger seems unworthy of a holy God. But his wrath is not the uncontrolled anger that we humans indulge in. It is God's holy anger against all evil, and everything that goes against his laws for humankind. God's wrath is his refusal to condone evil. It will be revealed at the final judgment, but is also revealed now in the present. It is stirred by all the godlessness and wickedness of human beings (verse 18).

Man and woman started in the highest possible position (Genesis 1:27; Psalm 8:5), but because of unbelief and disobedience they forfeited it and were banished from the immediate presence of God (Genesis 3:23–24). The story of Adam and Eve marks the distinct stages of decline in every human life.

The knowledge we possess

Just as we can recognize the work of a famous artist and identify music by our favourite composer, so we can see God's handprint on the world he made. We can know him in the power of the ocean and the delicate design of a snowflake; in the skill of birds who build intricate nests; in the arrangement of leaves around a stem.

These portraits in nature show us the wisdom and power of the eternal God. When we observe the glory of a sunrise or sunset with our physical eyes, the soul with its invisible eye may be deeply impressed by God's invisible qualities. In an open-air sermon, Paul said that God made the world in such a way that people would seek him and perhaps find him, as he is never far from any of us (Acts 17:24–28). Later on in Romans Paul writes that we do not need to search the skies or plumb the depths in our search for Jesus Christ, because he is as near as the word in our mouth and the faith in our heart (Romans 10:8–9).

God, then, has spoken to us clearly in nature, but we have closed our ears and eyes. This is our own fault, and we are 'without excuse' (verse 20). We are in a serious situation.

The knowledge we reject

When Paul says people 'suppress the truth' (verse 18), we must not imagine that they succeed. Rather, any attempt to restrain the truth about God is futile.

People reject, as well as suppress, the truth about God. Instead of praising God for his benefits, they ignore him. They live thankless lives, showing no appreciation of their tenancy of God's wonderful world. The immediate result of this rejection is found in their personalities: their thinking is futile and their emotions foolish (verse 21). Ironically, people claiming to have discovered the secret of life are really clueless about life.

The gospel says that the basis of a wise human life is pleasing God, but the foolish mind rejects God's rules as a basis for wise living. People sink to the depths of foolishness when they exchange the glory of God for images of animals (verse 23). The word for 'glory' in the original Greek suggests something weighty and substantial. To exchange something as substantial as the glory of God, revealed in creation, for something as insubstantial as images of mortal people and animals is utterly foolish. Read Isaiah's comment on those who exchange the God who 'carries' us for the gods who must be carried on the shoulders of the worshippers (Isaiah 46:6–7; 63:9). Reflect on the ways we as human beings give our foolish hearts to twenty-first-century idols.

Questions

1. How do you react to the idea of God's wrath? What does Paul mean by the term? How does wrath fit in with love?
2. If God has made himself so obvious to us all, why do so many people fail to believe in him? How do you think people try to 'suppress' knowledge of God in your society?
3. How does idolatry show itself in the world around us?

How might we be in danger of making even God into an idol if we have wrong ideas about him?

Paul's conversion

Paul's Damascus-road conversion is probably the most famous one in Christian history. Acts tells the story three times (9:1–31; 22:3–16; 26:4–18), and Paul refers to it in his letters (see 1 Corinthians 15:8–10; Galatians 1:12–17; Philippians 3:4–7; 1 Timothy 1:12–16).

He had been a fierce opponent of Christ and his church: he witnessed the stoning of Stephen and approved of his death (Acts 7:58; 8:1); he was responsible for imprisoning many Christians (Acts 8:3), and had a reputation for causing havoc (Acts 9:21).

Paul's conversion was not sudden. God had been speaking to him by pricking his conscience (Acts 26:14). Probably Paul had reflected on Stephen's words (Acts 7:1–56), observed the courageous faith of the Christians he had arrested, and studied the reports about Jesus that were in circulation. Perhaps he had even heard Jesus preach.

Paul's conversion should encourage us to pray that the most unlikely people might become Christians.

Romans 1:24-32

Wicked behaviour

When we reject God, moral evil is the inevitable result.

 The deliberate rejection of God is now followed by a set of frightening consequences. This next section of verses makes grim reading as we see God's holy wrath in action. Notice how the phrase 'God gave them over' appears in recurring stages:

▶ God gave them over to sexual impurity (verses 24–25).

▶ God gave them over to sexual perversity (verses 26–27).

▶ God gave them over to mental depravity (verses 28–32).

The phrase 'gave them over' suggests an intentional act. God exercises his wrath by giving people the very things they have set their hearts on – destructive things. The deepest addiction of the heart becomes the punishment. God permits people to be exposed to the terrible consequences of evil in order that they may turn and seek God's mercy. This was King David's testimony when he felt his bones had been crushed by the weight of a guilty conscience (Psalm 51:8). It was the experience of the prodigal son, who eventually made his way home (Luke 15:11–32).

As you analyse these verses, remember that God's present wrath is not his final word over people's lives. Do not ignore the bookends of grace that enclose this long section. Pray that some, after experiencing the judgment of God, will seek the God who saves us from us from his own wrath (1:17; 3:21).

God gave them over to sexual impurity

We cannot reject God and get away with it. We might imagine that his wrath in action involves turning people into pillars of salt or sending a plague of frogs on a nation (see Genesis 19:23–26; Exod. 8:1–15). Instead, his wrath is portrayed as letting people have their own way.

He lets us experience to the full what our foolish hearts most desire. If our strongest desire is to be immersed in illicit sex, he permits us to experience this sin and in time its effects become our punishment. The process is described as exchanging 'the truth of God for a lie'. If people persist in believing lies about God, in his wrath he 'gives them over' by confusing them in their thinking, and they practise a perversion of true worship by serving created things rather than the Creator himself.

Paul takes the example of the misuse of human sexuality in his society. Pagan temples in major cities might employ as many as a thousand prostitutes, who would offer sex for sale as part of pagan cultic worship. For example, farmers would visit the temples of fertility gods and goddesses such as Bacchus and Aphrodite, and participate in rituals that included sex with temple prostitutes, in order to ensure a good harvest.

Our society has its own ways of worshipping Aphrodite and Bacchus. Some people exchange the truth for a lie by believing that happiness is found in sexual fulfilment, perhaps involving pornography or promiscuous relationships. The truth is that God alone can satisfy our yearning for total unity with another. He has given us the joyful gift of sex, and clearly laid down its limits and purposes. But if we pursue sex as an end in itself, we shall discover that it leads us down a dead-end street.

If we exchange the truth about God's gift of sexuality for a lie, and worship the gift rather than its giver, God exercises his wrath. 'You will not believe the truth about me,' he says, 'so you must live with the consequences of giving your heart to something or someone who can never satisfy.

God gave them over to sexual perversity

Verses 26–27 concern lesbian and homosexual practices. They are mentioned not because they are worse sins than any other, but because they illustrate the theme Paul has been developing from verse 18. People make wrong choices. They exchange the real for the spurious (verse 23) and the truth for the lie (verse 25); now, the exchange is 'natural relations for unnatural ones' (verse 26).

Some suggest that in contrasting natural and unnatural relations, Paul may be thinking of those who by nature are homosexual, but who take part in heterosexual acts, which are unnatural for them.

Others think he is speaking only of exploitative homosexuality, which is unnatural, and that he is not condemning homosexuality as a whole, which the society of Paul's day considered natural. Fourteen of the first fifteen Roman emperors had been homosexual, and homosexuality was praised and regarded as higher than heterosexual love. In such a climate, it is said, Paul is speaking of sexual exploitation of younger men and women, which was regarded as unnatural.

The problem with such readings of the passage is that the text in 1:26–27 does not actually say either of these two things. Furthermore, the logical way to interpret the word 'natural' in this context would be to understand it as 'belonging to God's created order'. To act 'against nature' is to go against God's created order. In the context of this passage and the argument Paul has been developing, it cannot refer to what we as human beings may regard as natural or unnatural, according to our upbringing, cultural background or current lifestyle.

The key passages for understanding the term 'natural' are Genesis 1:27–28 and 2:18–25, confirmed and amplified by Jesus in Matthew 19:4–6. These passages indicate that God created male and female; sexual intercourse is intended for a husband and wife in marriage and no-one else, and what God the creator has joined together we must not separate. 'Natural' in this context means 'in line with the creator's intentions'. 'Unnatural' means 'contrary to his intentions'.

In addition, those from a Jewish background, like Paul, knew that the Old Testament law placed the homosexual act within the category of illicit sexual relationships, and that any breach of this law would put someone outside the covenant (Leviticus 18:22; 20:13).

Note two further things. First, sexual *orientation* is not the point at issue. The discussion centres on what individuals do with their sexuality. Secondly, we should be cautious about equating the 'penalty for perversion' (verse 27) with any specific outcome (such as sexual disease). Following the argument of the previous verses, we should take this phrase to mean that sexual perversion itself is the penalty for exchanging the truth for a lie.

Homosexuality is one of the most divisive issues facing Christians today, and we need a clear understanding of the Bible's teaching to help us minister to homosexual people. The booklet *Faith, Hope and Homosexuality* (Evangelical Alliance, 1998) affirms an orthodox view while showing sensitivity and rejecting homophobic attitudes. The chapter on same-sex partnerships in John Stott's *New Issues Facing Christians Today* (Marshal Pickering, 1999) is biblical and helpful.

God gave them over to mental depravity

This is the final example of what happens when people reject God and thereby face the consequences of his wrath in action. They do not acknowledge him in their thinking, so God gives them over to a depraved mind that lacks his wisdom, a mind so corrupted that it cannot be trusted to make moral decisions.

The twenty-one terrible things (verses 29–31) are examples of 'what ought not to be done' (verse 28) and make up a portrait of how people can behave when God gives them over to an unfit mind so that they even actually condone this behaviour.

Summary

This has been a long and complicated section, and we need to remind ourselves of the central theme before applying it to ourselves.

God reveals himself in two ways: in righteousness (verse 17) or in wrath (verse 18). If we reject him as the creator and saviour, then we must meet him as the judge. God abandons neither human beings nor the created universe, both of which remain the focus of his love. Even the revelation of his wrath is designed to turn our hearts towards his mercy. If we face his wrath, we are given over to what our hearts desire: what C. S. Lewis once described as 'enjoying for ever the horrible freedoms we have demanded'.

Questions

1. This section, 1:18–32, paints a bleak picture of human society. Is it really as bad as that? Is it worse? What are your reasons? Where do you see idolatry in your society? Read Psalm 139:23–24 slowly and reflect.
2. Read the list in verses 29–31 in a modern translation, or a paraphrase such as Eugene Peterson's *The Message* (NavPress, 1993). The chapter ends with a disturbing thought about approving of those who practise these things (verse 32). Is this as bad as the behaviour itself? Is it possible to make such behaviour respectable by condoning it? Give examples.
3. How can the church confront social disorder? Specifically, how can we confront sinners with the gospel but at the same time care for them pastorally?

Stop and look

Remember that this first section of Romans, up to 3:20, carries three emphases:

▶ All human beings are sinners.

▶ Sin brings terrible consequences.

▶ We need a Saviour to rescue us from sin.

Paul has begun his explanation of the gospel of God by presenting the bad news before the good news. He has divided the human race into four different groupings (the godless pagans, the upright moralizers, the outwardly religious and indeed the whole human race; see p. 44), and he confronts each group with the fact that they are sinners, guilty before God.

At the beginning of chapter 2, Paul embarks on a literary form known as a *diatribe*: he engages an imaginary critic in conversation. The critic poses a question or objection, and the writer proceeds to answer and demolish the objection. When Paul writes, 'You, therefore, have no excuse' (2:1), he is addressing this imaginary critic he has created for the sake of the debate he is about to unfold (2:1–16).

Romans 2:1–4

Blind spots about sin

We tend to judge others for the very sins we are guilty of committing ourselves. Paul warns that God's patience is not tolerance of sin but a period of truce that gives us chance to repent.

Paul identifies three blind spots about sin.

We condemn others while being lenient with ourselves

Some people might read the terrible catalogue of wrongdoing listed in 1:18–32 and, with an air of moral superiority, say, 'Amen to that, Paul.' Paul anticipates this by pointing out that what he has written about pagans applies equally to those who may think they have never done such sinful things. No doubt some would shrink from being identified with some of the sins mentioned in 1:18–32, but Paul says plainly that those who pass judgment on others are guilty of the very things they criticize.

'You … do the same things' (verse 1) may simply refer to plain hypocrisy. Many moralizers are blind to their own wrongdoing, but if they pause to think hard, there is ample evidence that they are guilty of the very things Paul has condemned in 1:18–32. This is particularly true if we think of the way Jesus included sins of thought as well as deed (Matthew 5:21–30). All of us are involved in sin and sinning, and no-one is excluded. God judges those who would judge others.

We think we can escape God's judgment

When we make human judgments, we tend to slant the evidence to cast ourselves in a favourable light. We magnify our strengths and minimize our faults. By contrast, God's judgment is based on truth (verses 3), and shows neither partiality nor favouritism (verse 11). Paul has already argued that sinful behaviour is a sign that the truth of God has been rejected in favour of a lie (1:25). He now suggests that judging others is sin, even though it may be a different kind of sin. If we set ourselves up as judges of other people, we have exchanged the truth for a lie (1:25) and have failed to honour the Creator.

We show contempt for God's kindness and patience

When God does not punish us immediately for our wrongdoing, we tend to assume it's because he is like an indulgent granddad. There was a saying in the Jewish wisdom writings: 'Even if we sin, we are thine.' People wrongly presumed that God turns a blind eye and that good behaviour cancels out bad deeds. Do we appeal to the riches of his kindness, tolerance and patience, forgetting their main purpose (verse 4)?

The Greek for the word 'tolerance' (verse 4) has links with the word 'truce'. God is exercising a truce towards sinners. He is being kind and patient towards our sinning to give us the time to reform our lifestyle and change our ways. The war is not over, but there has been a halt in proceedings, and God is holding back the fullness of his judgment in the hope that we will turn to him.

We sometimes don't realize that when God extends forgiveness towards us, it is intended to lead us to repentance (verse 4). Paul's Greek word for 'repentance' means a change of mind, and especially a change of attitude towards sin. Note the distinction between remorse and repentance that Paul makes in 2 Corinthians 7:10. If we are genuinely repentant, we will see the true nature of our sin and turn to Christ in our need.

Questions

1. In what areas of your own life can you detect the tendency to be critical of others while excusing your own failings? Ask God to show you.
2. Look at Jesus' teaching in Matthew 7:1–6. How can we obey his command not to judge (verse 1) while recognizing that some people ruin what is holy (verse 6)?
3. Think of situations in the world at large where hypocrisy about wrongdoing is apparent. Why was Paul so convinced, and emphatic, about God's coming judgment?

Romans 2:5–11

Sowing and reaping

God shows no favouritism. Those who have behaved in accordance with his will experience his blessing. Those who fail to do his will face his judgment. What we sow is what we reap.

Paul now spells out in greater detail the consequences of our response to God's kindness.

Stubborn hearts store up trouble for the day of wrath

The greatest obstacle to God's kindness and mercy is a stubborn and unrepentant heart (verse 5). These rare phrases convey the idea of a hardening of the heart ('stubbornness') and a refusal to forsake our sins ('unrepentant'). They should be understood by reference to the passages on the need for spiritual circumcision (Deuteronomy 10:16, and see the study on Romans 2:25–29). Stubborn and unrepentant hearts store up God's wrath for themselves, like deposits in the bank. This wrath will be revealed when the books are finally opened (verse 5).

God will give to each person according to what he or she has done

When God finally judges men and women, it will be a personal encounter ('each person'); and a specific, fair judgment based on what we have done. Those who work with God and co-operate with his purposes in doing good will receive eternal life. Those who persist in doing evil will be crushed by suffering and terrible anguish of heart. This judgment will include Jews and Gentiles alike, for God is not partial (verse 11).

Verse 6 quotes Psalm 62:12 and expresses teaching found in many parts of the Old Testament (see Proverbs 24:12 where it appears in question form). Jesus referred to God's rewards (Matthew 16:27), and Paul refers elsewhere to God's judgment and reward (e.g. 2 Corinthians 5:10).

Is Paul contradicting the heart of the gospel, that we are justified by faith in Christ alone, when he says we are judged by our deeds? By no means. But he does help us to see the important relationship between faith and works. While we are justified by faith, we are judged by our works. If we have decided to follow Jesus Christ and obey his teachings, this will be revealed on judgment day. If we have stored up works of stubbornness and unrepentance, this also will be made plain. Authentic faith will always generate good deeds. As James says, we demonstrate our faith by our works (James 2:18). Works do not compete with faith; rather, they should be signs of true faith at work.

What we set our hearts on determines our final destiny

Paul now draws a contrast between two fundamental orientations: the person who persists in doing good (verse 7) and the self-centred individual (verse 8).

Those who persist in doing good reproduce those qualities that come from a close walk with God: glory, honour and immortality. People like this will inherit eternal life in the very presence of God (verse 7).

Self-centred individuals are concerned only with pleasing themselves. They consciously repress the truth about God and practise evil habits. As a result, their lives will end in utter misery and anguish as God's final judgment comes on them (verse 8).

These two orientations illustrate the *harvesting* principle at work. What we sow we shall reap (Galatians 6:7–10). We must never become weary of sowing to the things of the Spirit, because in due time this lifestyle produces a harvest. This is why Paul refers in verse 7 to those who persist in doing good.

Paul repeats the very different outcomes of the contrasting orientations. Those who do evil will encounter trouble and distress (verse 9). Those who do good will find that it leads to glory, honour and peace (verse 10).

Jesus promised that those who persist in doing good will rise with him to enjoy his presence for eternity, while those who persist in doing evil will rise to condemnation (John 5:29). Surely we know from our own experience the sadness, misery and suffering that sin and evil bring us. This is contrasted with the gift of God's peace to those who seek his ways.

Verse 11 tells us that the terms of God's judgment are the same for everyone, whatever their background, because God has no favourites. The contrasting outcomes apply to both Jews and Gentiles (verses 9–10). The Greek word for 'favouritism' can suggest 'seeing only the masks people wear'. Because God does not show favouritism, he has the ability to see the true face behind the mask. He sees the face of blatant sins (1:18–32). He also sees the face of the moral hypocrite behind the mask of religious respectability (2:1–4). He will judge everyone fairly and impartially.

Questions

_____

1. In our modern world of instant access, overnight delivery and last-minute bookings, immediate satisfaction is something we come to expect more and more. Having to persevere at something is not very appealing. Think of Christians you know of, perhaps from the past or in other countries, who are examples of persisting in doing good. What sacrifices did they make?

2. If we are justified by faith alone, what does Paul mean when he writes that God gives to each person according to what he or she has done?

3. How do we know whether we are persisting in doing good, or being stubborn and unrepentant? Is it obvious to everyone, or only to ourselves?

4. Think about verses 4–5. If you were in charge of the universe, would you have judged the world *before* Auschwitz and Hiroshima could have happened, or would you have let them happen so that more people worldwide would have had a chance to repent?

Romans 2:12–16

The law written on the heart

The Jews have God's laws in a book. Gentiles, created in the image of God, have a moral law written on their hearts. This enables them to know something of God and his laws. His judgment of everyone is therefore fair and just.

 Is Paul being unfair to those who were not Jews by birth and background? As we shall see in the next study (on verses 17–29), Jews knew that they belonged to a spiritually privileged nation, and they let the world know that they saw themselves as an advantaged people. But shouldn't there be an equal-opportunities policy when it comes to judging people regarding their standing with God? What about the Gentiles who have never been privileged to share what God has given to the Jewish people?

Whatever our privileges, we shall be judged

The Gentiles stood apart from the law; they were given neither the privileges nor the responsibilities of Israel. The law of Moses, the Psalms and the words of the prophets, all of which pointed to the coming of the Messiah, were foreign to them. In one sense, they were under no obligation to obey them, since they were ignorant of them.

The Jews are under the law (verse 12), since they have been given the privilege of the full glory of God's revelation. Consequently, they are held responsible for their actions according to the law of Moses, which would be the basis of their judgment. The Gentiles would also face God's judgment, but on a different basis. We are judged according to the light we have received, and the basis of God's judgment is always fair and just.

Whatever our privileges, we owe God obedience

At first reading it might appear that Paul is teaching that we can be saved by good works, but, as he makes plain in 3:20, 'no-one will be declared righteous ... by observing the law'. That is, no-one can be declared righteous without keeping the law *perfectly*. The problem is that no-one is perfect.

If anyone was entitled to speak about this approach to God, it was Paul. The way of good works had been the pattern of his daily life for years. In fact, an extract from the writings of one of Paul's contemporaries (Rabbi Simeon, who was in fact the son of Paul's Jewish teacher) agrees with Paul on the need for obedience. It was not explaining the law that was the chief thing, he said, but doing the law. He warned against multiplying words, which could give an opportunity to sin.

On what basis does God find our behaviour acceptable? It's not because we possess a copy of the Bible or attend church to hear it explained in sermons. We can become serious students of the Bible, committing the Scriptures to memory and joining home groups devoted to Bible study. All of this is commendable, but the Word must first permeate our lives. Obedience to what God says is vital to our understanding of the gospel. We must listen to the Spirit of God as he seeks to make plain to us what we are reading. We must listen to the insights of others in the community of the church as we learn together, through the power of the Holy Spirit, to do what God's Word requires of us. In practical terms, this means that following Christ Jesus has profound implications for our lifestyle in the church and in the world (Romans 12 – 13).

The law written on the heart

Even though they lacked the written knowledge of what God requires of human beings, some Gentiles, some of the time, seemed to obey the commands of God by nature or by natural instinct. So when Paul uses the phrase 'a law for themselves', he is not using it in the way we would, to suggest lawless human beings who do their own thing. Rather, he sees that because Gentiles are created in the image of God, a limited knowledge of God is available to them.

When you observe the behaviour of some unbelievers, it is as if the requirements of God's law was written on their hearts. As if by instinct, they are honest in their business life, faithful in marriage, loving parents to their children, and compassionate to those in need. The Bible is full of examples of pagans who helped God's servants with acts of kindness: the town clerk in Ephesus (Acts 13:35), the Roman officers who helped Paul to escape (Acts 23:10), and the people of Malta who befriended Paul following his shipwreck (Acts 28:10).

The implication of Paul's argument is that if those who have not been given God's law have sufficient inward knowledge to do good deeds occasionally, this will be a basis for their judgment, when their good deeds will witness for them.

Every human being has the capacity to be guided by their conscience in making moral decisions and telling right from wrong. The conscience is not an infallible guide, and it varies in sensitivity from person to person. It can be trained to guide us (1 Corinthians 8:7; 10:25), but it can also be damaged by careless disregard for God's truth (1 Timothy 4:2).

We have been created with the capacity to experience what the Reformer John Calvin likened to the support of a thousand witnesses. We can be sustained and comforted by our good actions, but the conscience can inwardly torment and harass us when we do evil.

Paul's courtroom language – defence and prosecution – pictures people inwardly debating issues of moral conduct. He describes the thinking patterns we follow when making moral decisions. First, we know the law, whether Moses' law or the law on our hearts. Then our conscience gets to work, and finally we think and decide what to do.

Sometimes this triple process motivates us, or accuses us, into righteous action. At other times it will both ignore the law and deaden the conscience in order to justify, or defend, our actions.

Whatever our privileges, we face a day of judgment

On the day God has appointed, Jesus Christ will carry out a just and fair judgment (16). It will be a searching judgment because God alone knows all our secrets. He knows our hearts and understands out motives (1 Chronicles 28:9). He can search the heart, and knows everything about us as human beings (Jeremiah 17:10). Jesus reminds us that nothing is hidden from the sight of God, and our heavenly Father who sees in secret is able to reward us accordingly because he knows the true state of the heart (Matthew 6:4, 18). The Jews will be judged by revealed knowledge. Gentiles will be judged by the triple law we have just described. Our consciences will bear witness to things we have kept secret.

From 1:18, Paul has been developing his theme that all people are guilty sinners before a holy God. He now concludes that although Gentiles do not have a written law like the Jews, they do possess a law, written on the heart, that gives them sufficient knowledge of what God requires, and by this they will be judged. God has finalized the day and selected his judge (verse 16).

Paul refers to 'my gospel' (verse 16) to emphasize the personal responsibility he accepts as an ambassador to whom God has committed the message of reconciliation (2 Corinthians 5:19).

Questions

1. 'What about those who have never heard?' is an objection raised against Christianity time and again. How would you respond to this? If you are studying in a group, practise your reply in pairs, or hold a debate.

2. The Jewish people were to tie the commandments on their foreheads and write them on their door-frames (Deuteronomy 6:9). Paul speaks of the law being written on righteous Gentiles' hearts. How can we allow God's Word to permeate our lives? Try to think of specific ways we can immerse ourselves in it more deeply.

3. What particular aspects of God's law do you, your home group and your church need to think about more deeply?

Romans 2:17–29

People with spiritual advantages

Although the Jews are in a privileged position as God's people, the Jewish members of the Roman church must not put their trust in traditions and ceremonies alone. These are meant to be signs of an inward faith; they have no saving power.

 Paul's approach is now upbeat. He seeks to persuade his readers to consider a very different kind of righteousness. He confronts those things on which people base their spiritual confidence, and reveals them to be false bases for righteousness with God.

He challenges a wrong understanding of the Jewish tradition (verses 17–18); a wrong attitude to Jewish teaching (verses 19–24); and a wrong confidence in Jewish ceremonies (verses 25–29).

A wrong understanding of the Jewish tradition

Paul reacts against the self-righteous attitude he knew so

well. Prior to his conversion he would have set great store by his Jewish heritage, relied on his keeping the law and boasted about his special relationship to God (see Philippians 3:4–6). But now that he had gained Christ, the things he was so proud of in his Jewish tradition took second place.

It is true that the Jews were a very privileged nation. God had chosen them from among all the nations to be his people. He had revealed to them his law, the standards he expected of them. As a nation, they had superior knowledge of his will. But the purpose of spiritual advantages was to deepen their love for God and appreciation of his grace, not to breed self-righteousness.

These Jews had forgotten the purpose of God's promise made to their ancestor Abraham, that through him and his descendants all the families of the earth would share in spiritual blessings. Prophets such as Micah warned them that they must not take spiritual advantages for granted (Micah 3:11–12). John the Baptist repeated the warning (Matthew 3:7–9). Jesus challenged Jewish people to guard against placing false reliance on spiritual privileges (John 8:39). We too need to guard against misusing the spiritual privileges of a Christian background and make sure that we lay a solid foundation in the knowledge of Jesus Christ as Saviour and Lord.

A wrong attitude to Jewish teaching

The spiritual privileges given to the Jews were meant to be a blessing to the 'foolish' and the 'infant' mind. The Jewish teachers Paul addresses considered themselves guides to the blind, bringing intellectual light to those in the darkness of ignorance. But these guides had withdrawn from the world, the very place where they were meant to offer wisdom, and the light of knowledge was failing to shine. Instead of setting an example and following God's moral law, they were guilty of hypocrisy. They saw themselves as teachers, but they were not applying their own teaching to themselves.

Paul selects four areas to illustrate his concern: money (verse 21); sex (verse 22); idol worship (verse 22); and dishonouring God (verses 23–24).

Money

The law of God included plain teaching on the proper use of money, and Jesus endorsed it in his own ministry. The house of God, the temple, had been seriously misused as a place of worship and had to be cleansed by Jesus (Matthew 21:12–13). Greed for money meant that some preyed on poor widows in the hope of gaining monetary advantages (Matthew 12:40).

Sex

The law was also clear on sexual matters, especially the issue of divorce. Jesus condemned those who found a way round the law to suit their own convenience (Matthew 5:31–32), and he amplified the law's teaching on adultery to include not only the physical act but the lustful attitude (Matthew 5:27–28), of which the self-righteous may well be guilty.

Idol-worship

The question in verse 22 about robbing temples may refer to actual robberies of pagan temples and the sale of their treasures for profit. Perhaps some of Paul's readers had no hesitation in condemning the worship of idols, yet were willing to gain materially by selling or purchasing goods stolen from idol temples.

Dishonouring God

The most serious failure is reserved till last. By wilfully disregarding the need to live out God's law as well as teach it, they were bringing the name of God into disrepute. The double standards of these Jews in public life prompted onlookers to blaspheme the Jews' God.

As Christians we have a fuller revelation of what pleases God, and we have a greater inward power (the Holy Spirit) enabling us to keep his commands. We need to check that what we profess with our lips is matched by our lifestyle.

A wrong confidence in Jewish ceremonies

Circumcision was vital to the Jews. It was the sign that a male Jew had been admitted to the covenant (Genesis 17:9–14). Failure to be circumcised meant exclusion from the covenant family. Circumcision was a badge of privilege and a passport to salvation. Such was the confidence of the Jews in the sign of circumcision that they had memorable sayings to reinforce this sense of spiritual security. A well-known rabbi in the time of Paul said, 'Circumcision saves you from hell', and 'Abraham sits at the gates of hell and no circumcised Jew is allowed to pass him.'

Paul challenges this false confidence in circumcision. He admits that the rite has value, but only for those who keep God's law (verse 25). Any circumcised Jew who fails to keep the requirements of the law is no better than a Gentile sinner (1 Corinthians 7:19). He then suggests something quite shocking: an uncircumcised Gentile who pleases God by observing his laws may be reckoned as a member of the covenant people (verses 26–27). You can imagine the faithful waving Exodus 12:43–49 in front of Paul and asking him if he had read it recently!

Paul is telling his Jewish readers that they must live out what the symbol signifies. The outward, visible ceremony of circumcision in the flesh is a sign of an inward, invisible work of the Holy Spirit in the heart (verses 28–29). In the act of physical circumcision, something is cut away by a knife and removed. In the work of spiritual circumcision, things are 'cut away' by the work of the Holy Spirit. This inner work was spoken of in the Old Testament (see Deuteronomy 10:16; Ezekiel 36:26–27; Jeremiah 9:25). The theme of inner circumcision by the Holy Spirit will be developed in 8:4 and especially in chapters 12 – 16, where the outward signs of the inner work are seen to be a vital part of Christian discipleship.

The issue of circumcision may seem irrelevant to us Christians today, but we must never imagine that our baptism alone is a badge of privilege or that our membership of a prestigious church is a passport to salvation. Any outward ceremonies must be accompanied by the inner working of the Holy Spirit. The Spirit alone can produce that inner disposition of love which shows itself in a life of service to God.

Questions

1. In what ways can reputation and status be a snare to Christians?
2. Luke 18:9–14 illustrates Paul's teaching here. Imagine that the Pharisee is genuinely thankful to God as he prays, and turn him into a church warden, elder or minister. Then retell the story in a modern setting, and discuss the results with others.
3. Given the outreach and witness of all the Christians in your community, why doesn't that community take the good news of Jesus more seriously? Can you identify any obstacles Christians have placed in the way of people who might otherwise be interested in Christian faith? How could they be removed?

Circumcision

Circumcision is an operation to remove the foreskin of the penis. Israel was not the only nation to practise this ritual, but, for the Jews, circumcision had deep significance. It was a sign of the covenant God had made with Abraham (see the studies on chapter 4; also Genesis 17:11 and Exodus 4:24) and of belonging to the covenant people. In other parts of the Scriptures the external rite is explained as an outward sign of an inner work performed by God (Deuteronomy 10:16; 30:6). The Jews of Paul's day were meticulous about observing the command, but Paul reminds them that circumcision is useless without love for God and his laws (2:25–29).

Since the coming of Christ, it is not necessary for Christian men to submit to the rite (Colossians 3:9), although early believers from a Jewish background struggled to come to terms with the implications of this (see Acts 15:3–21; Galatians 2:1–14). Our 'circumcision' as believers is spiritual and is closely linked with Christian baptism. In our union with Christ Jesus in his death and resurrection, we put off the old person and put on the new person we are in him (Colossians 2:9–12).

Romans 3:1–8

Strong questions about God's character

Being a circumcised Jew does not put you right with God. So what are the advantages of belonging to the chosen people?

The Old Testament tells us that God particularly chose Israel to be the bearer of his light to the other nations. He gave the Jewish people gracious gifts such as a covenant binding himself to them, laws to obey that reflected his character, and circumcision as a visible sign of the special relationship Israel enjoyed with God.

It now appears to Jewish listeners that Paul is setting aside the differences between Jews and Gentiles (see 2:17–29). The particular relationship between God and Israel and the gracious gifts he has given to the Jews now seem to count for nothing. In the words of the opening question: is there any advantage in being a Jew (3:1)?

Much hangs on the answer to this question, as their belief in God's faithfulness is being challenged. Paul begins to answer these objections here in chapter 3 (and will return to a fuller account in chapters 9 – 11).

This section repeats the diatribe style we met at the beginning of chapter 2. It is set out in the form of a question-and-answer dialogue. This literary method was familiar to first-century readers.

Paul may have been drawing on his vast experience as an open-air evangelist, repeating the questions the hecklers may have thrown at him. His answers may also reflect his inner wrestling with questions of faith when he first became a Christian. Read Philippians 3:4–11 for a reminder of Paul's testimony.

He addresses four questions:

1. *What is the advantage of being a circumcised Jew?* This is a real dilemma for the Jewish mind. Is God now setting aside all he purposed to do through one nation over hundreds of years? Even circumcision appears to count for nothing (verse 1).

Paul disagrees, and reminds his readers that the Jewish people have been given a very important privilege. They have been charged with the guardianship of the Holy Scriptures – a high responsibility. Nothing that Paul has said will remove this blessing, but not even this high responsibility can put them right with God. It is a privileged blessing, but does not entail right standing with God. This comes only by faith, and the Old Testament Scriptures testify to this principle (read about the life of Abraham in chapter 4).

2. *If Jewish people do not believe what is written in their Scriptures, surely this doesn't mean that God will abandon them?* The second question from the imaginary heckler concerns God's faithfulness. Paul has said that the Jews have been entrusted with the very words of God (verse 2). This includes all God's promises recorded in the Old Testament. But if the people to whom the promises were made don't believe them, does this reflect on the faithfulness of the

God who made the promises (verse 3)?

This is unthinkable, says Paul. God never breaks his word. Even if every human being failed to tell the truth, so that the lie became a pillar of the state, God would remain true (verse 4). The quotation from Psalm 51:4 records David's experience; he found God to be faithful and true when he owned up to his own lying and faithlessness.

3. *If you're right that uncircumcised Gentiles are acceptable to God, we may as well sin boldly to bring out more of the love of God. What does that say about God's justice in punishing sinners?* The heckler in the crowd is getting bolder with his questions. He now throws in the idea that faithless, lying behaviour is excusable because it provides a great opportunity for God to demonstrate his love. The more sinful we are, the greater the good news. If God loves us this much, why does he judge human beings (verse 5)? What kind of justice is that? If God is unjust, he is unfit to rule the world and judge the human race (verse 6).

This idea that God might act unjustly is another unthinkable position for Paul. The words translated 'Certainly not!' (verse 6) are very forceful – 'Never in a million years!'

4. *Are you saying that the more we sin, the more God can forgive us, and this brings greater glory to him? You can't be serious!* The heckler's reasoning here is that it doesn't matter if we lie because it enables God's truth to shine forth, and his glory is increased. There is no need to condemn sinners, as their sins provide more opportunities for God to show how loving and gracious he is (verse 7). It has even been reported that Paul is preaching on the theme 'Sin boldly and see how much God forgives you' (verse 8).

This final question from the imaginary heckler is so contemptible that Paul's answer is crisp. The questioner has descended to the depths of slander. This idea is so outrageous that Paul will not demean himself by arguing against it (verse 8).

While these particular questions may seem strange to our thinking today, we should note that Paul takes people's questions about God seriously. If we want to engage in evangelism with integrity, we must give clear answers to questions about faith.

Questions

1. The Jews read the Torah with great care and respect (for example, people are not supposed to touch the pages, and if a copy is damaged it must be buried rather than destroyed). Similarly, Muslims will never place a copy of the Qur'an on the floor. Should we copy their example in our treatment of the Bible? If not, why not?
2. Does confidence in God's grace lead to complacency about sin? How can we avoid this?
3. Paul takes these questions very seriously – all except the last one. How does his example help us in our evangelism?

The law

Paul uses the term *law* in various ways in Romans. It appears seventy-two times, underlining its importance in his thinking. It usually refers to the law of Moses, in the Old Testament. Paul also writes of the law of sin (7:23) and of people who are a law for themselves (2:14). It is best to interpret the word in its context each time.

God's law functions in four ways.

▶ *The law is a mirror* (James 1:22–25). It shows us what righteousness is, and, if we look carefully, how unrighteous we are. The mirror can only show us what we are like; it is powerless to change us.

▶ *The law is a restraint* (Romans 13:3–4). Because the law is good and spiritual, it can support those who want to restrain the wicked and protect the poor.

▶ *The law is an agent provocateur* (Romans 7:7). The more we see the KEEP OUT notices, the greater our desire to go in. The law can stimulate us to do wrong things.

▶ *The law is a revelation* (Romans 7:12; 8:1–4). It shows us God's character and purposes. God expects us believers to fulfil his law in the power of the Holy Spirit who lives in us. As we love God with all our heart, soul, mind and strength, and others as ourselves, we fulfil the law.

Romans 3:9–20

The whole world is guilty

The whole human race, Jew and Gentile alike, is guilty before God. All are helpless under the power of sin and need to be liberated by God.

Paul has adopted the role of counsel for the prosecution in a court case which began in Romans 1:18 and continued until 3:8. Like a skilled barrister, he has carefully built his case, with supporting evidence, that every human being is a guilty sinner before God. Absolutely no-one is excluded from this charge; Jew and Gentile alike are guilty. Now he comes to his summing-up speech.

Every human being is under the power of sin

Jews and Gentiles make up the whole human race, and without exception they are 'under sin'. This important phrase conveys sin's power over people. This is the first of forty-seven occasions on which Paul uses the word 'sin' in Romans. (He will explain it more fully in 5:1–21.) In this verse, sin is described not as wrong behaviour or bad thoughts, but as a tyrannical dictator who controls all human beings, who are helpless slaves under sin's power. Our only hope is for liberation (7:14–25).

In verses 10–17, Paul 'strings pearls', as the rabbis termed the stringing together of Old Testament verses to make a point. Paul's point is that humankind is universally sinful. He may have been using a ready-made list of proof-texts, or he may have carefully selected these verses from the Psalms, Ecclesiastes and Isaiah.

The verses fall into three sections.

▶ *Verses 10–12* present a dismal picture of the human race. Every human being without exception is 'under sin'. 'No-one ... not even one' is without sin, Paul's texts stress repeatedly.

▶ *Verses 13–14* illustrate the way sin dominates our speaking: we lie, curse and say bitter things. The description of the throat as an open grave underlines that sin is deep-seated, and the comparison with poisonous snakes reminds us of James's teaching on the power of the tongue (James 3:1–12). We know from our personal experience that what people say can do untold damage to others. In this context, Paul is illustrating the all-pervasive power of sin.

▶ *Verses 15–18* show how the power of sin extends to other areas of conduct which involve the wrong use of the human body. Instead of offering their bodies as living sacrifices for God's service in order to bless others (Romans 12:1), people ruled by sin commit acts of violence and bloodshed, and don't know how to make peace. Jesus wept over Jerusalem because the city did not know the way of peace (Luke 19:41–44). This section closes with a reminder that every sin we commit flows from a disregard of God and that the essence of all sin is ungodliness (verse 18). If the fear of the Lord is the beginning of all wisdom (Proverbs 1:7), those who have no fear of God are not even on the starting-blocks when it comes to living in a way that pleases God.

God's law condemns all, both Jews and Gentiles

Paul quotes verses outside the first five books of the Bible, the section of the Old Testament normally referred to as 'the Law'. The quotations in verses 10–18 indicate that he is widening the term 'law' to mean the whole of the Old Testament. Living under the law (verse 19) and observing the law (verse 20) mean perfectly obeying what the law commands.

But because of the pervasive power of sin, no-one will ever be declared righteous in God's sight (verse 20). This way of trying to be right with God is impossible not only for the Jews, whose aim was to obey the laws of the Old Testament perfectly, but also for Gentiles, who have some knowledge of God from creation and the natural law God has written on their hearts, but who fail to acknowledge God in their thinking (1:19–20; 2:14–15). And because the law *addresses* all, it *applies to* all.

The way we know we have sinned is by becoming aware of God's standards and measuring ourselves against them. As we read the commands of the law we become conscious of sin (verse 20). One translation renders the latter part of verse 20: 'It is the straight edge of the law that shows us how crooked we are.' When we read God's laws in the Bible, they are not meant to be a cure themselves. They are powerless as a rescue plan. Rather, they are intended to show us the truth about ourselves and our helplessness under the power of sin.

The accused are in the dock and are given the opportunity to speak in their defence. The defendants choose to remain silent, because the evidence that has been presented is overwhelmingly convincing. Every guilty mouth may as well be silent, for the whole world is accountable (verse 19).

A passage that may help us understand these verses is Mark 15:5. Jesus stands as the silent defendant before Pilate, the judge. Pilate is amazed because Jesus chooses to remain silent. We know that from his baptism to his cross, Jesus took the sinner's place, as our substitute. Therefore his silence before Pilate is a picture of the silence in which we must stand before God, the judge. Our silent recognition of our personal accountability as sinners is the best preparation for the good news of the gospel, to which Paul now turns.

Questions

1. Look up the verses in Paul's list and read them in context: Psalm 5:9; 10:17; 14:2–3; 36:1; 140:3; Ecclesiastes 7:20; and Isaiah 59:7–8. What do you make of this analysis of humankind?
2. Think of an incident or situation that made you suddenly aware of how powerful sin is. Why do you think we become complacent about sin?
3. 'There is no-one righteous, not even one.' Who do you think of as righteous? How would it affect your faith if that person committed an unthinkable public sin? Do you think we should be more open with one another about temptations and sins experienced in private? How? Pray for your Christian brothers and sisters.
4. Why do people expect Christians to be 'good'? Are we any different from them? How? In what ways does this affect our relationship with them?

Romans 3:21–26

The heart of the gospel

In one of the most important sections of Romans, God reveals his way of making people righteous, a free gift received by believing in Jesus Christ.

Paul has demonstrated the fallacy of a belief popular in every generation: that if we try hard and are reasonably good, a loving God will see us right. We can  surely enter heaven by being kind to our neighbours and doing occasional good deeds. If God ignores the good things we do, he is unjust and cannot claim to be a God of love.

A million times 'No!', cries Paul. There is something radically wrong with human beings and no amount of good deeds can put this condition right. We need God himself to intervene with a rescue plan. After the first three chapters of bad news, what a relief to read the words 'But now', which are the prelude to some good news for every human being! This rescue plan has the following features:

- ▶ It comes from God (verse 21).

- ▶ It is not new; the Old Testament law and prophets testified to it and revealed that this good news has always been in God's plan and purpose (verse 21).

- ▶ We receive it through faith alone in Jesus Christ (verse 22).

- ▶ It exactly matches our need (verse 23).

- ▶ It is a free gift from God (verse 24).

- ▶ It is the fruit of Jesus' sacrifice on the cross (verse 25).

By using these pictures, Paul shows us what God has done through his rescue plan.

Lawcourt: the guilty are acquitted or 'justified'

Paul repeats what he has shown in the previous chapters: people without exception are guilty before God (verse 23). In God's court the verdict has been announced and the sentence has been passed. We deserve to die, but, incredibly, we are justified freely (verse 24).

Slave market: the slaves are set free or 'redeemed'

Sin is not just something we do, nor is it only an attitude of mind. The Bible describes sin as a power that can control us. The word 'redemption' is usually used in connection with slavery (Romans 6:6–7). Paul has in mind the familiar story of the Israelites when they were slaves in Egypt. They were set free by trusting in lambs' blood that had been sprinkled on the doorposts of their houses (Exodus 12). This deliverance became known as the Passover, because the judgment had 'passed over' their families. The thought here is that Christ in his death is our Passover Lamb. He has paid the terrible price for our freedom as slaves. We experience redemption from the slavery of sin through Jesus Christ (verse 24).

Temple: the sacrifice is accepted and our sins are atoned for

The phrase 'sacrifice of atonement' in verse 25 is drawn from the Old Testament temple services in which animals were sacrificed to atone for sin. Jesus is our sacrifice, and, by his death, not only has the record of our sin been wiped out, but God's wrath has also been removed (1:18).

There are two sides to Christ's atoning work. There is something in God, as well as in us, that has to be dealt with before there can be peace between the two parties. The 'something' on God's side is much more serious than the 'something' on our side. God shows his love clearly in this atoning sacrifice (1 John 4:10), and without his powerful intervention there is no rescue plan.

Why did God wait?

Paul also tackles a question that must have been in his readers' minds: if what God has done is such good news for human beings, why didn't he do it earlier?

Paul's reply is that God was awaiting the 'right time' in human history to demonstrate that he was both just and merciful (verses 25–26). Cynics may have brought charges against God's character, suggesting that for many hundreds of years divine righteousness appeared to be asleep. With the exception of Noah and the flood, it would appear to the human mind that sin in Old Testament times had been covered rather than punished. But the spiritual mind sees this as a waiting period reflecting God's patience towards the human race. He was planning a new creation through Jesus Christ, whose sacrificial death proved that God was righteous because in it sin was punished and sinners were justified: all without compromising the holy character of a just and merciful God.

Questions

1. Why do you think we seem to prefer to work our way to heaven than to accept God's rescue plan?
2. Think of another Christian church or denomination with which you have differences. Then read again the end of verse 22 to verse 24. How should this affect our relationship with other Christian groups?
3. Try to turn the 'story' of this paragraph into a courtroom drama, with the defendants (verse 23), witnesses (verse 21b), accusers (verse 24) and of course judge and jury (God himself). Can you see how it could be done – and presented to others?

We are made right with God by grace alone, in Christ alone, through faith alone. there is no room for boasting or distinctions between Christians. Those who live by faith demonstrate their love for God by keeping his laws.

The faith factor has been central to the preceding verses. On three occasions Paul underlines the necessity of faith: *righteousness* comes through faith in Jesus Christ to all who believe (verse 22); *atonement* is received through faith in his blood (verse 25); those who have faith in Jesus are *justified* (verse 26). He now explains more about this faith factor, indicating that it leaves no room for boasting (verse 27) or distinctions between Jewish and Gentile Christians (verse 29), and that walking by faith involves keeping God's laws (verse 31).

Paul resorts again to using the literary device of the imaginary heckler in the crowd, who asks a difficult question. There are three such questions, and Paul has an answer for each challenge.

No-one must boast

The Jews were proud of their national identity and their personal righteousness, and believed that this gained them merit with God (see Matthew 3:9–10; Romans 2:17, 23). Gentiles also were capable of boastful attitudes (1:30). The first question from the heckler (verse 27) concerns those who boast that God owes them something as a reward for the kind of life they have lived.

Paul emphatically repudiates this idea. All human

boasting is excluded. When the heckler throws in a supplementary question about the grounds on which boasting is excluded (verse 27), Paul's reply underlines the principle of faith. How can you boast about a gift you have received and did not deserve?

Anything about us that is good in God's sight we have received from him as a gift (1 Corinthians 4:7), and if we are going to boast, we should boast about the Lord and not ourselves (1 Corinthians 1:27–31).

No-one must discriminate

In the second question (verse 29) the heckler is asking who is entitled to the gift of faith. Is Paul saying that the good news of the gospel is for Gentiles as well as Jews? If so, this is not what we have been taught as Jews. The Gentiles have no share in our spiritual blessings.

God had chosen the Jewish people and given them privileges not granted to other nations (see 3:2; 9:4–5). Some Jews were proud of what they saw as their exclusive relationship with God. But Israel's privileges were never intended to discriminate and exclude. Paul has to confirm this second principle of faith, which states that God is the God of Gentiles as well as of the Jews (verses 29–30). God's promise to Abraham was that through his descendants the *whole world* might be blessed (Genesis 12:2). Furthermore, as every Jew would have to affirm, there is only one God (verse 30; see also Deuteronomy 6:4), and what he requires of Jews and Gentiles alike is faith. Faith alone in Christ alone is what counts.

This was a major issue for the early church. The Holy Spirit had to lead Jewish Christians to see that God's gift of salvation was freely available to all who put their faith in Jesus Christ. God has no favourites between Jews and Gentiles, as Peter learned in Acts 10 – 11. Our racial background, religious traditions, gender and social grouping count for nothing at the foot of the cross, where all those expressing faith in Jesus Christ may come and find equal mercy (Galatians 3:28).

No-one must set aside God's law

The heckler's third question (verse 31) concerns the goodness of God's law and the requirement on Christians to obey these laws. Is Paul teaching that faith sets law on one side? If so, can't we disregard God's laws and commands?

Not at all, responds Paul. Once again, he has to explain that the function of the law was to reveal the nature of sin and expose our helpless state under its power. God's law was never intended to be the cure for sin, but to lead us to cry out to the divine doctor for healing (Matthew 9:12).

When we become Christians, our eyes are opened to see that God's law is holy and his commands are good (Romans 7:12; 8:4). The law leads us to see our need of Jesus Christ, and those who put their faith in him as Saviour and Lord are enabled to uphold the requirements of God's law. Our aim is to live a life of faith that works to keep God's laws and commands. Those who live by faith in the Son of God are empowered to live a fruitful life by the power of the Holy Spirit (Galatians 5:22–23).

God did not introduce this faith factor suddenly; it is as old as Abraham. Paul is now going to tell the story of this Old Testament character, whose life of faith pointed to the Messiah who was to come. Jesus himself commended Abraham's faith: 'He rejoiced at the thought of seeing my day' (John 8:56).

Questions

1. What can (1) you; (2) your church; and (3) the church worldwide be proud of?
2. In what ways do we exclude others from our fellowship? Have you ever been excluded yourself? How did you react?
3. What do you understand by the phrase 'God's law'? In what senses do you think Paul meant it in verse 31? (Remember that he does not require Gentile Christians to obey, for instance, the food laws of Deuteronomy 14 and Leviticus 11.)

Atonement

To make atonement means to make amends, literally to make 'at one'. In the Bible the term describes the process by which God deals with sin and restores our relationship with him.

In the Old Testament, sins were atoned for through the sacrifice of an animal. Priests would offer the blood (which was very closely associated with the life of the animal; Leviticus 17:11), and through this the people's sins would be forgiven. The burnt offering made atonement (Leviticus 1:4) as also did the sin offering and the guilt offering (Leviticus 4:20; 7:7) and supremely the sacrifices offered on the Day of Atonement (Leviticus 16). The instructions for the sacrifices on this solemn and important day are rich in detail and are worth studying for a better understanding of the Old Testament background of the concept.

The New Testament continues to emphasize the seriousness of sin. Understanding who Jesus is enlarges our understanding of atonement. Christ offered the perfect sacrifice on the cross (Hebrews 9:26; 10:5–10). He paid the penalty for our sins (Galatians 3:13). He took our place and died our death (Mark 10:45; 2 Corinthians 5:21).

The source of all this is God's love for us (John 3:16; Romans 5:8).

Romans 4:1–3

Abraham as an example of faith

The faith principle: Abraham believed God and this was counted to him as righteousness. So he models the person who has faith in God's promises.

 The principle of faith has been central to Paul's writing in chapter 3. He chooses this Old Testament example of justification by faith because Abraham was the founder of the Jewish faith and a model example of a believer. If it can be proved that Abraham knew the principle of justification by faith, this will have a significant impact on his readers. Paul has already explained that the law and the prophets testify to this right standing with God which comes through faith in Jesus Christ (3:21), and now he chooses the greatest of the patriarchs as further evidence from Scripture.

Abraham's significance

We are invited to consider what Abraham discovered in this matter of knowing God (verse 1). Paul introduces Abraham as 'our forefather', and later in the chapter will refer to him as 'the father of us all' and 'our father' (verses 16–17). Abraham is notable as someone who found favour with God because he trusted the promises God made to him (Genesis 15:6). In a sense he serves as a prototype for all believers, and his experience is meant to be an example for us to follow (verses 23–24).

In order to understand how Paul uses events from the life of Abraham to illustrate his teaching, you will find it helpful to read about four key moments in Abraham's life story in the book of Genesis.

In *Genesis 12:1–9* we read of God's call to Abram (as he was then) to leave his home, and his promise to him that all the peoples of the earth would be blessed through him.

In *Genesis 13:14–17* God made Abram a further promise, that his offspring would be as numerous as the dust of the earth. This promise was made when he and Sarai were childless, and was repeated in Genesis 15:5, where the Lord promised that the offspring would be as numerous as the stars in the sky. It is in this context that the crucial words are recorded: 'Abram believed the LORD, and he credited it to him as righteousness' (Genesis 15:6).

In *Genesis 17:1–17* the names of Abram and Sarai were changed to signify their parenting of many nations, and circumcision was given as a sign of the covenant God had made. We read of the repeated promise of God that they would have a child, a humanly impossible event by this time, as Abraham was a hundred and Sarah was ninety.

Finally, in *Genesis 22:1–18*, the promise had been fulfilled and the miracle son had been born. God now tested Abraham by asking him to sacrifice his son Isaac. When Abraham complied, God again confirmed the promise of descendants as numerous as the stars in the sky and the sand on the seashore; through this offspring (or seed) the whole world would be blessed. (Read Galatians 3:16 to see how Paul understood Abraham's 'seed'. You will also find it helpful to read Hebrews 11:8–12, 17–19.)

Abraham's works

From the Scriptures we learn that Abraham was known as the friend of God (Isaiah 41:8), and that God told Abraham's son, Isaac, that his father had 'obeyed me and kept my requirements, my commands, my decrees and my laws' (Genesis 26:5).

In the Jewish tradition, Abraham was a hero. It is important to know how he was revered in order to understand the meaning behind the phrase 'justified by works' (verse 2). The Jews recognized Abraham as someone who had kept the law of God before it had been given to Moses. He was such a good man that he knew instinctively what pleased God. Jews were taught to believe that Abraham was 'perfect in all his deeds before the Lord'. Some believed that, along with Isaac and Jacob, Abraham was 'one who had never sinned against God'. The Jews suggested he was the perfect example of the righteous man of Psalm 1.

Paul would be well aware that both the Scriptures and Jewish tradition gave ample support to those who said that Abraham with his good works had plenty to boast about (verse 2). Paul knew that some rabbis taught that God's favour to Abraham was a reward for his perfect observance of God's laws. But to concede that Abraham was *justified* by his works would be to lose the central theme of justification by *faith* that Paul has been elaborating from 3:21.

Paul concludes that Abraham may have had plenty to boast about before other people, but not before God (verse 2).

Abraham's faith

Paul now quotes the proof-text from Genesis 15:6 which declares that Abraham enjoyed right standing with God, not on account of his good works, but because he simply trusted God's word: 'Abraham believed God, and it was credited to him as righteousness' (verse 3). The key words here are 'believed' and 'credited'. Abraham was justified because he simply believed, not because he *did* anything. In the passages from Genesis listed above, the point of the story surrounding the promise of a child is that Abraham was helpless to do anything – but he stood by the promises God had given him. He believed God against all hope (verse 18) and without weakening or wavering in his faith (verses 19–20). Abraham is the best example of the gospel principle that God freely gives and faith receives the gift.

The second word in the verse, 'credited', appears several times in this chapter and is drawn from the world of accountancy. It means to reckon something to someone's account whether that person deserves it or not. Paul expands this dual meaning of the word 'credited' in verse 4. He uses the same word when writing about Onesimus, Philemon's runaway slave: if Onesimus owes Philemon anything, says Paul, he is to 'charge it to me' (Philemon 18). Here in verse 3, it is clearly meant to indicate that Abraham had not *earned* the right to have his account credited with righteousness, but that God had *freely given* Abraham an unearned gift of grace that was credited to his account as righteousness.

The rest of chapter 4 will unfold different aspects of Abraham's faith and their abiding lessons for us today. Keep in mind the central theme of his story. Faith is simply taking God at his word. Faith looks at the difficulties in the light of all that God has promised. God freely gives and faith receives his gift.

Questions

1. Who are your role models, your heroes, the people you look up to in the faith? What is it about them that inspires you?
2. Try putting the phrase 'justification by faith' into your own words. Perhaps you could design an Easter card that expresses the message of 'justification by faith' as clearly as possible.
3. If faith is simply taking God at his word, what has he promised us? Reflect on the fact that Abraham's faith flourished first when he was facing childlessness, and then when God told him to sacrifice his child.

Romans 4:4–25

Faith believes God's promises

Many believed that Abraham was a good man, but the controlling factor in his life was that he believed that God had the power to do what he had promised. We Christians are invited to imitate this faith ourselves.

Jewish Christians who came to faith in Jesus Christ had of course been brought up to read the Old Testament from a Jewish perspective. No-one better than Paul understood the need to take familiar Old Testament stories and reinterpret them in the light of all that God had accomplished in Jesus Christ. Gentile Christians also would benefit from this teaching as they came to see that justification by faith was not something new that came with Jesus Christ, but something as old as the patriarch Abraham.

Jewish Christians would be very aware of the significance of circumcision as a mark of the covenant, and of the vital importance of observing the law with a life of good works. These three important features – circumcision, law, and works – are the background to these verses. Paul wants to demonstrate that although Abraham was circumcised, observed the law of God and performed good works, he was pre-eminently a man of faith. This is why he is an example for Christians.

The passage is divided into the following four sections: Abraham and good works (verses 4–8); Abraham and circumcision (verses 9–12); Abraham and the law (verses 13–17); and Abraham a man of faith and an example to follow (verses 18–25).

Abraham and good works

We have seen from verses 1–3 that Abraham had many good works of which to boast before other human beings, but never before God. We saw the importance of the word 'credited' (verse 3), and now Paul begins to explore the meaning of this word further.

Someone who works for an employer deserves a wage. This is an employer's obligation. If you work, your account is credited with your wages and they can never be considered a gift (verse 4). Because Abraham did not work (that is, he did not trust in his works to put him in the right with God), God was not obliged to credit his account with a wage. But because Abraham trusted God's promises (that is, he did not present himself to God as a worker deserving a wage but trusted that he would receive a free gift), his faith is credited as righteousness (verse 5).

As a further illustration of God's justifying the wicked (verse 5), Paul now calls on King David to present written evidence from one of his psalms. In Psalm 32 we read of someone who is guilty of sin and deserves to be punished (verse 7). In accounting terms, this person's account should be debited till it is in the red. Instead, God's gracious gift credits the person's account with forgiveness so that it is in the black. As the psalm says, this person's transgressions are forgiven, his sins are covered and his sin will never be counted against him (verses 7–8).

In summary, justification by faith means that we cannot offer good works as a means of earning righteousness; rather, God credits us with righteousness as a free gift, and faith receives the gift (verse 4–5). Justification by faith also means that we sinners, who do not deserve forgiveness, are credited with righteousness as an undeserved gift, and God does not count our sins against us (verses 6–8).

Abraham and circumcision

Are the blessings of justification by faith for the circumcised only or for the uncircumcised too (verse 9)?

To a Jewish audience this was an important question, and Paul will answer from the life story of Abraham. God gave the covenant mark of circumcision first to Abraham (Genesis 17:9–14). An uncircumcised Jewish male was not considered a proper Jew, and the rule was that 'no man must eat the Passover without the mark of Abraham in his flesh'.

But under what circumstances did Abraham receive the blessings of the righteous? Was it before or after he was circumcised (verse 10)? Abraham was not circumcised until fourteen years after he had responded in faith to God's promise (Genesis 15:6; 17:10–14). He was counted as righteous in God's sight on the grounds of his faith, not of his circumcision (verse 11). His circumcision was an external sign of an inner faith that pre-dated the ceremony of Genesis 17.

Because his faith preceded his circumcision, Abraham may be considered the father of all who believe (verses 11–12). He is the father of uncircumcised Christians because he demonstrates that circumcision is not essential to faith. He is also the father of those circumcised Christians who are put right with God through faith, just as Abraham was before he was circumcised.

Abraham and the law

If God's promise to Abraham preceded the sign of circumcision, it also preceded the giving of the law to Moses – by 430 years (Galatians 3:17). Wanting to help those readers with a Jewish background to reinterpret the Scriptures from a Christian standpoint, Paul shows the contrast between the law and the promise. The former has to be strictly observed, while the latter is freely received as a gift.

Some rabbis taught that God gave Abraham the promise because he observed the law. They said that his law-keeping was rewarded with the promise of his son Isaac.

But if this was true, his faith had no value and God's promise was worthless (verse 14). God promised Abraham a child, and his faith believed it. This promise was expanded to include the pledge that through his offspring Abraham would become the father of many nations (Genesis 13:14–17). This explains the phrase 'heir of the world' (verse 13), which has now been fulfilled in Christ and in the worldwide Christian family: through Christ 'the world ... the present or the future ...' are all ours as Christian believers (1 Corinthians 3:21–23).

As Abraham's offspring, we can follow in our father's footsteps by believing in the God who creates life out of the dead – even out of nothing – and who fulfilled the promise of a child out of Abraham's old body, which was as good as dead (verses 17, 19).

Abraham, a man of faith and an example to follow

In Hebrews 11, Abraham is named among those who are commended for their faith in God's promises. In this final section we learn from Abraham's life what faith really is.

Abraham believed against all hope that God would give him the long-promised son (verse 18). He was promised the largest family imaginable – as numerous as the sand on the shore and the stars in the sky – when it seemed impossible that his wife could have even a single child. It was, on the face of it, preposterous. There was certainly no hope in his human circumstances; his body was as good as dead with regard to reproduction. After all, he was approaching his hundredth birthday, and his elderly wife Sarah was well beyond the time when she could conceive a child (verse 19).

Instead of hoping in circumstances, he placed his hope in what God had said would happen. He looked to the one who can give life to the dead and bring things into being that did not previously exist (verse 17). He believed that God could visit his dead body with life, and was fully persuaded that God could do what he had promised (verse 21).

During the period of waiting for the promise to be fulfilled, his faith must have been severely tested. We know from the book of Genesis that he had questions for God (15:2); that Sarah did not always understand what God was doing (18:1); and that he was called by God to offer the promised child, his beloved son Isaac, on the altar (22:1–2). Amazingly, through all this, Abraham's faith did not waver, but was actually made stronger. Such faith always brings glory to God (verse 20).

We have had more than an ancient-history lesson in these verses (23–24). Abraham believed God's promises to him; now, we should have faith in the one who was delivered over to death for us and raised to life for us (verse 25).

Our faith is in the God who called a universe into being out of nothing. He called Isaac from the deadness of Abraham's body; he called Jesus from the tomb; he has called us from the deadness of our sins to walk in newness of life; and he can breathe life into the dead bones of his church. That is a God in whom to believe.

Questions

1. What good works, rituals and rules are we expected to follow as Christians? If we follow Abraham's example, what must we do to become righteous?
2. Have there been times when praying for something really stretched your faith? How did God answer your prayers? Is there something God is asking you to have faith for now?
3. Some people have suggested that, because Abraham was justified without hearing of Jesus, or having faith in him, he represents the possibility that followers of other religions may be 'justified' before God without becoming Christians. What do you think? Would Paul agree or disagree? Why?

Justification

'Justify' is a legal term meaning 'acquit'. It includes the idea that there is no further condemnation.

To justify someone is to pronounce, accept and treat him or her as a just person. The justified person is not liable to any penalty, and becomes entitled to receive all the privileges of the just. 'Justification makes no actual change is us; it is a declaration by God concerning us' (D. Martyn Lloyd-Jones).

Read Deuteronomy 25:1 for a concise Old Testament picture that explains justification. See also Proverbs 17:15 and Romans 8:33–34.

Read the following passages in Romans:

▶ Justification is God's gift (3:24).

▶ We receive it by faith (3:21–31).

▶ Christ's death achieved it (5:9).

▶ It forgives and blots out our sin (4:7–8).

▶ It brings us peace with God (5:1).

▶ It immediately gives us the status of God's children (8:14–16).

▶ It includes the gift of the Holy Spirit, whose life in us gives us a foretaste of the life to come (8:17, 23).

Justification is the complete forgiveness of our sins and the permanent status of children of God, with all the blessings associated with this status.

THE NEW LIFE

Romans 5:1 – 7:25

Stop and look

Paul has being steadily building a logical argument from chapter 1, with these steps:

▶ The whole world is guilty before a holy God (chapter 1).

▶ No-one can be saved by good deeds – not even the best life is good enough (chapter 2).

▶ God alone can save us, and we experience this salvation by his grace through the gift of Jesus and of faith in him (chapter 3).

▶ This way of faith was not new with the coming of Jesus – it was present in the lives of Old Testament believers, of whom Abraham is the best example (chapter 4).

To apply chapters 1 – 4 to ourselves:

▶ We need to be justified – put right with God.

▶ We *can* be justified by accepting God's gift of grace through faith.

Now we come to the beginning of chapter 5, which assumes that the great event of becoming Christians is behind us. The first two verses describe the blessings of being Christians (verses 1–2). The rest of the chapter deals with questions that arise in most people's thinking soon after becoming Christians:

▶ Why do I continue to experience suffering if I have been put right with God? Will this relationship last? Will God ever give up on me, especially if I am not leading a perfect life? (See verses 3–11.)

▶ What is so special about me, that God should share his life with me? Surely only very holy people can count themselves among the privileged? (See verses 12–21.)

Romans 5:1–2

The blessings of being Christians

Being right with God involves past, present and future blessings. Justification is not the whole of the Christian life, but the whole of the Christian life follows from justification.

Read the 'Stop and look' section on the opposite page first, to see where we are in Paul's argument, before looking more closely at these two crucial verses.

Paul's 'Therefore' (verse 1) assumes that those he addresses have received and are enjoying God's gift of justification by faith, which he has so carefully explained in the first four chapters. Here now are three great implications of justification by faith.

We have peace with God

We have been reconciled to God through the death of his Son. This does not mean that we are set free from anxiety to live a stress-free life, but that God has changed his attitude towards us. When we failed to keep his laws we were his enemies (verse 10). Now we are justified, he calls us his friends (John 15:13–15). God has made us members of his family. The spiritual battle is over, the internal conflict has ceased, and peace has been declared.

There are tangible ways of knowing we have begun this new relationship with God. We stop being afraid of God, and of death, and experience a conscience at peace with itself. Whenever our conscience does condemn us and a voice inside says, 'You cannot be a true Christian if you behave like that', the way back is not to work on our emotions but to remind ourselves of our justification. Peace with God does not depend on feelings.

We have access to grace

The word 'access' means 'introduction'. Jesus has given us a personal introduction to fellowship with God the Father and with himself (1 John 1:3). We have access to all the blessings of knowing God because Jesus shed his blood (Hebrews 10:19–22). One definition of this 'grace' (verse 2) is 'God's Riches At Christ's Expense'.

It's good to reflect on the great benefits of this open access that we enjoy as we spend time in prayer and meditation on the Scriptures. The Bible tells us that the Lord shares family secrets with those who have access to his presence (Psalm 25:14): we can gain understanding in how the Lord is praying for his church in its witness to the world (John 17), and we can begin to see how the Lord prays for us when our faith is put to the test (Luke 22:31). These are some of the privileges of access.

We have the hope of glory

Two types of hope are mentioned in these verses. There is the hope of faith, which develops as we consider who Jesus Christ is and what he has done for us. It comes to life when we think about the truth that 'the Son of God ... loved *me* and gave himself for *me*' (Galatians 2:20).

As we grow in the Christian life, we come to know the second type, hope based on experience (see the following study on verses 4–5). Sometimes as we follow Jesus we may feel it is like a winter's day. But just as on the coldest day the sun can shine, so in the most difficult of circumstances we can see the glory of God breaking through.

Questions

1. Grace. Have you ever been introduced to, or had special access to, someone famous or important? How did this make you feel? Think about our open access to God, a far greater privilege, and how this thought can enhance and inspire our prayer times.
2. Peace. What does peace with God mean? How should this understanding affect our relationships with other Christians?
3. Hope. 'I hope you get the job.' 'I hope we won't have long to wait.' What is the difference between 'hope' in sentences like these, and Paul's 'hope of the glory of God'? How does this 'hope' help us to 'rejoice'? Pray for Christians around the world who face opposition for their faith, that they may be able to rejoice in this hope.

Romans 5:3–11

Positive attitudes to suffering

If I suffer, does this mean I am not truly a Christian? What positive value does suffering have for me? When I struggle as a Christian, does it cast doubt on the reality of my faith?

The New Testament unanimously agrees with Paul's apparently unbelievable words, 'we ... rejoice in our sufferings' (verse 3). See Acts 5:40–41;  16:22–25; 2 Corinthians 12:9. Does this mean we have been invited to belong to the stoical 'grin and bear it' brigade, the stiff-upper-lip, 'never shed a tear' society, or the 'smile even when you're hurting' fellowship?

A thousand times *no!* This would be a lie, and Jesus has called us into a fellowship of truth.

The answer lies in the phrase 'we know' (verse 3). We can rejoice in our sufferings as believers because we know something. We have inside information. When we gain access to the Father, he shares with us his wisdom about whatever happens to us, and this brings greater insight. This insight does not tell us *why* something has happened, nor does it give us a clear view of its outcomes (1 Corinthians 13:12). But it helps us to develop positive attitudes to suffering. Hundreds of years before this letter was written, the psalmist affirmed the same truth (Psalm 119:67, 71).

God helps us to persevere in suffering

Paul links our suffering with perseverance (verse 3). This word suggests patience and steadfastness.

In parts of the world where the church is persecuted,

some Christians may be called to persevere in faithful suffering to the point of death (Revelation 2:10). However challenging our situation, we are invited to consider that perseverance in times of suffering does us more good than trouble can do us harm.

Next we see how Paul links perseverance with our character (verse 4). As we persevere in the Christian life our faith is tested and proved. When we are called to persevere, God uses these periods to test the quality of our faith. Christians are like precious metal refined through the fire of a furnace (Zechariah 13:9; 1 Peter 1:6–7). When we are passing through extreme difficulties we need the assurance that God is with us in our time of trial, vividly described by Isaiah as an overwhelming flood or an uncontrollable fire (Isaiah 43:1–2).

God can use the experience of adversity to build our character as believers. In a time of suffering and adversity we can learn something about

▶ the way we can wisely handle the setbacks of life,

▶ the fickle friendship of the world,

▶ the malice and destructive power of Satan,

▶ the kindness and sympathy of Christian believers, and

▶ the wisdom, love and power of God.

The final link in the chain is that between character and hope (verse 4). When we survive the flood and the fire of an ordeal, we become aware that we have passed through a test of our faith. The lessons we have learnt strengthen our hope. It becomes obvious (sometimes more to others than to ourselves) that God is reproducing in us the image of his Son Jesus Christ. He does this by the pouring his love into us by giving us his Holy Spirit (verse 5).

God's plan for a Christian lifestyle is set out plainly in the Bible (see Matthew 5:1–10; Galatians 5:22–23; James 3:17; 2 Peter 1:5–9), and the Holy Spirit, as the power and presence of Jesus himself, enables us to see these lifestyle changes in our own personalities. When we perceive this work of the Holy Spirit in action, even through extreme suffering, it produces hope that we shall share God's glory.

God assures us that he accepts us

But that hope doesn't always come instantly. It is easy to feel that God has rejected us and does not love us. Besides, how do we know that 'the hope of glory' is not just wishful thinking? What happens when we find ourselves struggling as Christians? Does this cast doubt on our faith?

When we return to the place where all Christians know they are loved – the foot of the cross – we become more sure that God has accepted us. Consider what kind of person you were before you became a Christian: you were power-less, ungodly, a sinner, subject to God's wrath, and God's enemy (verses 6–10).

Now think what God has done for you in Jesus Christ: he has poured out his love into your heart, he has given you his Holy Spirit, he works to a flawless timetable on your behalf, his Son Jesus Christ gave his life for you, and you are reconciled to God through Jesus' death and saved through his resurrection life (verses 5–10).

God proves his love for us

If God loved us so much when we did not deserve it, how much more he must love us now that we know him!

Paul illustrates his point from friendship (verse 7). All but the exceptionally courageous among us would quickly dismiss the thought of sacrificing our life for someone we hardly knew. We might think long and hard about risking our life for a warm-hearted friend. But when Jesus laid down his life for us on the cross, we were unattractive and undeserving people. If God justified us while we were his enemies, there are no limits to what he will do for us now that we are reconciled to him as his friends (verses 10–11). Jesus' death and resurrection prove that he loves us with an everlasting love, whatever the circumstances. No nagging doubts can stand before such amazing love.

Questions

1. What is your experience of suffering? How did you cope with it? Pray for anyone you know who is suffering in some way.
2. Discuss or think of people who have laid down their lives for others. If someone were to do this for you personally, how would this affect the way you lived?
3. Compose a brief letter or phone call to a Christian couple who have just lost a child through famine or sudden illness. In what ways would you use Romans 5:1–11 to bring comfort to them?

Suffering

Although Paul notes some of the benefits of suffering (5:1–5), suffering is still a hard experience for Christians, bringing many doubts and feelings of rejection. Suffering exists because we live in a fallen world, where sin abounds. Pain and heartache are an integral part of life on this earth. As Christians, we are set apart from this world in the sense that as God's children we don't go along with all its ways. But, because we live in this world, we are not free from pain and sickness, sin and death.

As those who have stepped out in faith, we will face trials of many kinds simply because we are Christians (1 Timothy 3:12). Paul says that we were destined for trials (1 Thessalonians 3:3), and Peter reminds us that Christians in many parts of the world suffer to the point of losing their lives because of their love for Jesus (1 Peter 5:9).

We also know that in all things God is always working for the good of those who love him (Romans 8:28), and pain and suffering are certainly included in 'all things'. We must look forward with joy to the hope that will not fail us, and believe that God will work in our lives, through the bad times as well as the good.

Share in your group some personal stories that illustrate that although Christians are not immune to tribulation or tragedy, God gives us the grace to come through our trials victoriously.

Read Romans 8:28–39, and talk through the things that threaten to separate us from the love of God.

Romans 5:12–21

Ruined and rescued

One man and his sin ruined the human race. One man rescued us from the ruin of sin and death. The blessings of the reign of grace in Christ far outweigh the ruinous effects of the reign of sin and death in Adam.

Paul is presenting the story of the human race as a play in two acts. Act 1 is about Adam, the disobedient man who ruined life for all his descendants and made it impossible for us to escape sin and death. Act 2 describes Christ, the obedient man, who rescued the human race and made it possible for us to enjoy the blessings of God's grace. Although Adam is named only in verse 14, he is the man Paul has in mind throughout the passage. The story in Genesis 3 is the one to read as background.

The passage may appear difficult at first glance, and one way to grasp the meaning is to understand the shape of this section. The story of Adam starts (verse 12a) ; the partnership between sin and death is clarified (verse 12b); and there is further clarification of the place of the law in Adam's story (verse 13). Paul then suggests the comparisons and contrasts between Adam and Jesus Christ (verses 14–17); he resumes what he began to say about Adam and states again how Adam and Jesus Christ differ (verses 18–19); and finally, there is a further reference to the law (verse 20) and a concluding word on the triumphant reign of grace (verse 21).

Paul breaks off his introduction to Adam in verse 12 and resumes it in verse 18. For this reason some translations put brackets around verses 13–17. In these intervening verses Paul deals with the vast differences between Christ and Adam.

▶ *Through Adam comes the partnership of sin and death* (verse 12). Through Adam's disobedience, sin entered the world. Death then used sin as an entrance door into the world. Adam's disobedience involves the whole human race in a 'sin and death' situation from which there is no escape, apart from the rescue plan effected by Jesus Christ. Every human being sins and every human being has to suffer death as the consequence of sin. This is traceable to the actions of Adam.

▶ *Before the coming of the law, the seriousness of sin is proved by the presence of death (verses 13–14)* Some may have protested: 'how can you claim, Paul, that "all have sinned" (verse 12), when it is only by the *law* that sin can be clearly defined?' Paul's answer is that sin was in the world before the law was given to Moses. The fact that sin was 'not taken into account' (verse 13) does not imply that it did not matter, or was not punished. The fact that people died in the period between Adam and Moses is a sign that the wages of sin were being paid (6:23). The phrase means that sin was not the clearly defined thing it was under the law. It took the law to expose the full seriousness of sin.

How Adam is like Christ

The one comparison that can be made between Adam and Christ is that both of them, by a decisive act, determined the destiny of the human race. Adam disobeyed God, and, by his one sin, many experienced death. Christ obeyed God, and, by his one death, many experienced life. It is in this sense – the one act affecting the many – that Adam is described as a pattern of the one to come (verse 14). Because of this comparison, Christ is sometimes referred to as 'the last Adam' (1 Corinthians 15:45–49).

How Adam is very unlike Christ

Paul begins to draw a stark contrast between Christ's gift and Adam's trespass (verse 15). Adam's single act of disobedience led to the death of many. By contrast, Christ's act of obedience is described as 'the gift that came by the grace of the one man, Jesus Christ'. The effect of this gift is an overflowing abundance of grace to many people.

Next Paul shows the results of each single act. In Adam's case, judgment and condemnation followed one sin. By contrast, the gracious gift of Christ followed the countless sins of the centuries and led to justification (verse 16). This means that every sin committed by every human being in every period of time is covered by this one act of grace. Amazing grace!

Paul now contrasts death and life (verse 17). Adam's solitary trespass was the entry point for the terrible tyrant of death, with its mastery over every human being. When death reigns unchallenged, it has a killer sting and reigns victorious (1 Corinthians 15:55).

By contrast, the 'how much more' abundance of grace makes us like members of a royal family (8:17). Through his mighty resurrection, Christ has drawn the sting of death and reigns victorious over the grave. Because of our right standing with God, we share in his mighty reign in life. We can experience the justification that brings life to all (verse 18), and rejoice in Christ's obedience, by which we have been made righteous (verse 19).

The passage concludes with a word on the law. Jewish readers would be shocked to discover Paul denigrating the role of the law and suggesting it had the power to provoke sin. But it did. We know from the story of Adam that God's prohibition actually encouraged Adam and Eve to see something desirable in what had been forbidden. When the law was added, the trespass increased. The law was unable to prevent sin or rescue us from it.

Another rescue plan was required. Thanks be to God, the increase of sin brought the increase of grace. So abundant is this grace that it is described as a 'reign'. This is the final contrast between Adam and Christ. Sin's reign has been replaced by the reign of grace (verses 20–21). How do we know we are living under the reign of God's grace? Because God has brought us into right standing with himself; that is his grace is reigning through righteousness (verse 21). All these blessings of eternal life come to us through the last Adam, Jesus Christ our Lord.

Questions

1. Reread Genesis 1 – 3. Why did Adam's sin have such far-reaching consequences? To what extent does our own sin have similar results?
2. If the law had the power to provoke sin, why did God give it to his people? See Galatians 3:19–26.
3. How can we counter the effects of sin and the fall in our society?

Romans 6:1–7

Sharing in Jesus' death and resurrection

Does Paul's emphasis on the grace of God encourage people to sin with gusto in order to receive more grace? Our union with Christ in his death and resurrection makes this unthinkable.

The suggestion that sinning with licence gives God more opportunity to display his grace is total nonsense, retorts Paul (verse 2). It betrays little understanding of the radical change that has taken place in Christians. Paul feels strongly about this suggestion because it is totally incompatible with this change.

We have died and been raised

When Jesus died on the cross, he not only died to free us from our sins (as our substitute); he also died there in our place (as our representative). Because of this, Christians accept Christ's death and resurrection by faith as their own (2 Corinthians 5:14–15), and symbolize this in their baptism. Our baptism is the sign of a death, a funeral service and the beginning of a new life. We are incorporated into a dynamic union with Christ Jesus. This means that becoming a Christian is not like deciding to become a member of a club with new interests, new friends and new commitments (though we have those too).

Rather, when by faith we share in Jesus' death and resurrection, an old era has died and been buried and a new era has begun. We now enjoy the closest possible relationship to Jesus, and we are meant to experience his power both to forgive us and to deliver us from sin. Because believers have died to sin, it is impossible to go on living sinfully as though this death had never taken place. The rest of this chapter explains the meaning of this phrase in verse 2.

It is important to grasp what Paul means here by the word 'sin'. Paul is not saying that Christians suddenly become perfect and are never tempted to make the kinds of mistake that are unworthy of their new position as children of God. Paul recognizes that although it is still possible for Christians to sin, there has been a radical change in their attitude to sin. Every believer must realize that the old way of life is over and a new way of life has begun. Paul uses two pictures to explain this.

In our baptism, we shared in Christ's death and resurrection

You must understand the meaning of your baptism, says Paul. God has given us baptism to signify our living union by faith with Christ Jesus. By our baptism in water we are united with Jesus in his death, burial and resurrection. We go down into the waters (death), are plunged beneath them (burial) and rise up from them (resurrection). The phrase 'baptised into' (verse 3) further indicates the close personal relationship we enjoy with Christ. Through our baptism we are marked as belonging to him. Being under his ownership as his servants, we must reflect the likeness of our Master. If our old way of life, ruled by self, is dead and buried, we shall strive in his power to obey him and thus demonstrate the new way of life, under the lordship of Christ (verses 4 – 5).

Our death released us from sin's dominion

Paul now presses home the meaning of our death with Christ. Our baptism signals a new life of obedience under Jesus' command. So we should expect to see major changes in our lifestyle, reflecting our new way of life.

Some think that the death of 'the body of sin' (verse 6) means that Christians are entirely dead to the influence and attraction of sin. This is a false interpretation. Consider your personal experience of temptation and failure; the testimony of other Christians and their desire to lead a holy life; the teaching of Scripture (e.g. Matthew 6:12; Romans 7:14–25; James 3:2; 1 John 1:8); and the meaning of verses 12–13 in this chapter. All these remind us that Christians are not dead to sin's attractions.

Look at verses 6 and 7 in stages to understand what has died.

There has been a death

Our old self was crucified with Christ (verse 6). This old self is not our pre-conversion *nature*, but our pre-conversion *life*: that is, our membership of Adam's family (5:19). What we were before we became Christians is what has been crucified with Jesus. The death is unique and unrepeatable. Compare this with Galatians 5:24, where the death is continuous and repeatable as we are called to take up our cross daily. Our old life has died, and now we must die to sin daily.

There has been a sabotage

The body of sin has been rendered powerless (verse 6). This refers to the body in which we live, which in itself is not sinful, but has been used as the instrument for sinful behaviour.

God created our bodies. Jesus was born as a human being and he was raised with a resurrection body. God intended us to love and serve him in our bodies, which are temples belonging to him (1 Corinthians 6:19–20). The problem is that our self-centred nature has been at the beck and call of sin, and in this way our bodies have been under the rule or dominion of sin. But our death with Christ has sabotaged this relationship to sin. We are no longer at the beck and call of our sinful desires. That way of life is over. The selfish nature has been deprived of its ultimate power to rule our lives.

There is no more slavery

We are no longer slaves to sin (verse 6). Our old, pre-conversion life as the helpless slaves of sin is now dead and buried. Our union with Christ in his resurrection means that a new power is present in our bodies, so that sin can no longer use our minds and bodies over whenever it desires. We are no longer helpless slaves under sin's dominion, but have the power to live under the direction of the Lord Jesus Christ.

There are no debts to pay

Anyone who has died with Christ has been truly freed from the slavery of sin (verse 7). Death pays all the debts and cancels all the obligations. If we died in union with Christ and have been raised to walk in his ways in the power of his resurrection, we are set free from the dark powers of Satan. He can no longer come knocking at our door, pretending we still belong to him. Our response should be: 'The person you are looking for has died, and this house is under new ownership.'

Questions

---

1. Think about how you would naturally respond to

   ▶ a company that persistently makes mistakes in your account;

   ▶ someone under you at work who ignores your instructions time and time again;

   ▶ a child who is constantly disobedient.

   Is it right to forgive and forget time and time again? How do these relationships differ from our relationship with God?

2. How do you remember your baptism, or first public profession of faith? If it is helpful, compare your life

before your death with Christ, and your new life. Thank God for what he has done.

3. What does it mean to be united with Christ? Read the passage again, noting the different ways we are 'with Christ' or 'united in Christ'. How do we (or how should we) express this 'union' in everyday life?

Antinomianism

The question in 6:1 alludes to a mischievous heresy called *antinomianism*. This teaches that we can go on sinning as much as we like, expecting God to forgive us freely. The word *antinomianism* comes from two Greek words, *anti* (against) and *nomos* (law). It refers to those who have rejected the law as binding on conduct, a position found both inside and beyond the church.

The early church would have been aware of everyday sayings such as 'Eat, drink and be merry' (see 1 Corinthians 15:52). In the second century, heretics suggested that the law did not originate with God, but with a demonic being; therefore Christians were not obliged to keep the law.

Some might have been suggesting that Paul's statements in 3:8 and 5:20 opened the door to this misunderstanding. The belief that we can sin boldly because God forgives freely is a dangerous distortion that has threatened believers in every age (Jude 4). Paul responds vehemently to the suggestion that we can carry on sinning but escape its penalty of sin: 'By no means!' he says (6:15). Later, in 12:9–21, he will demonstrate that his ethics, like those of Jesus in the Sermon on the Mount (Matthew 5 – 7), conform to the law of the Old Testament. The difference lies in Jesus' and Paul's emphasis on our inner transformation by the Holy Spirit, who enables us to keep God's laws. (See the studies on chapters 7 – 8.)

As you read these verses, remember to acknowledge the weakness in all of us that makes light of our failures and assumes God's tolerance towards sin. 'Antinomian' is not just a word for heretics.

How might the gospel encourage people to sin more than ever?

Do we excuse our own failures on the ground that God will forgive us?

Romans 6:8–14

The body as God's servant

We are to think of ourselves as dead to the power of sin and alive to the power of God, ready for his service alone. This is a call to a once-for-all dedication to Christ as well as a daily offering of our bodies in the service of God.

Our faith is anchored in the fact that Christ Jesus died and rose again (verses 8–9). This was a unique, once-for-all event and there is no question of its being repeated (verses 9–10). Our union with Christ in his death and resurrection gives us confidence in God's work in our own lives. When God commands us to become what he has made us in Christ, his victorious work in Jesus makes us confident that he will complete the work he has begun in us too (Philippians 1:6). We are to work out the resurrection life of Jesus in our practical experience, and verses 11–14 underline that our ethical endeavours are essential to Christian growth.

Something to recognize

The way Christ's death and resurrection should shape our thinking and our living requires serious thought. Our union with Christ is a fact of faith and not a feeling. Paul's phrase 'count yourselves ...' (verse 11) invites us to act upon something God says is true. He says in his Word that we are dead to sin and alive to God in Christ Jesus. Being dead to sin does not mean we are sinless. We are dead to the reign and rule of sin in our lives, but this does not indicate that we will never experience temptation and failure. There will be setbacks and disappointments, but God has anticipated these and has provided a way of escape from temptation (1 Corinthians 10:13) and a way of forgiveness when we sin (1 John 1:8–10).

But when we do have these experiences of falling back into the old way of being influenced by the power of sin, we are acting out of character. This is not normal behaviour for Christians. Read Colossians 3:1–4 as a helpful passage alongside verse 11.

Something to resist

We are to resist any desire to give the old slave-master a foothold in our lives (verse 12). Paul is saying, 'Don't behave as though the old slave-master of sin owned you.' Organize a revolution in the name of your rightful owner! Because we share in the resurrection life of Christ Jesus, we have a choice when the power of sin begins to exert its influence. Before we became Christians we were helpless to resist the power of sin, not least because we were spiritually dead (Ephesians 2:1–3). But we are no longer helpless, and we have the power to make a choice. We will not offer our bodies as tools for sinful behaviour. This reference to the mortal body and its links with evil desires (verse 12) does not mean our bodies are sinful. But it warns us that our old sinful nature, even though it has been robbed of its total power to rule us, is still able to use the parts of our body. We must resist this evil use and not place ourselves at the disposal of sin. Evil desires have no place in the life of those living under the lordship of Christ, and they must be resisted (James 4:7).

Something to offer

We have already seen that when Christians offer the parts of their bodies in the service of sin, they are acting out of character. Here in verses 13–14 is positive encouragement to make another kind of offering: a once-for-all presentation of ourselves to God when we are baptized (6:1–4), and a daily offering of the parts of our bodies, as well as our talents and abilities, as tools by which God can build his kingdom of righteousness (12:1–2). We are all called as disciples to see our bodies as temples through which God's glory shines in a broken world (1 Corinthians 3:16).

Questions

1. How many times does Paul mention death or dying in this passage? What ideas and associations does this bring to mind? How does this help you to understand Paul's point?
2. Why does Paul have to remind us not to obey evil desires? If God has done the amazing work of setting us free from sin once and for all, how will Paul's simply telling us make a difference? Surely we can only be either free or not free?
3. How can the church help us to use our talents and gifts as instruments of righteousness?

Romans 6:15–23

A tale of two masters

Paul pictures two slave-masters. We have been set free from slavery to sin and are now slaves of God. There is no middle way. Either we serve sin or we serve God.

Does the gospel encourage sin? If we emphasize the way of grace, do the floodgates of sin open (verse 15)? This is an inevitable question after all that Paul  has said about the supremacy of grace and the impossibility of salvation through keeping the law. It must have seemed to some of Paul's readers that because he was rejecting the *law*, he was therefore encouraging people to sin. Paul pauses in the flow of his teaching and deals with this major misunderstanding. In chapter 7 he will unpack the relationship between Christians and the law in more detail. In this section he addresses a single issue: who is your slave-master? Is it sin, or is it God?

The illustration of slavery appears inappropriate and unsuitable, and Paul apologizes for using it (verse 19). It is inappropriate, because many of his first-century readers will have had first-hand knowledge of this humiliating and degrading social practice, and the reference could appear insulting and insensitive. It is unsuitable because the imagery of slavery fails to describe the freedom and joy of the Christian life. But Paul adds an explanation to his apology. He has to use startling imagery to help those who are weak in their understanding (verse 19). They have a foolish tendency to miss the point, thinking that the freedom of the gospel promotes freedom to live as you please, with no moral responsibilities (verse 15).

In the slavery illustration, Paul finds the ideas of total

allegiance and accountability. This is just as true of the relationship of sinners to the slave-master called sin, as of believers to their slave-master, God. This is a tale of two masters. And Paul makes it abundantly clear that we serve the one or the other. There is no third way. We are slaves to the master we obey, and there are only two masters in this life: sin and God (verse 16).

Although Paul does not use the name of God in verse 16, he does so in verse 22; and the ideas used in this chapter – slaves to grace (verse 14); slaves to obedience (verse 16); and slaves to righteousness (verses 18–19) – all point to the contrast between the two masters. If we refuse God's lordship, we are under sin's mastery. Sin deludes us when we imagine that we are independent beings, free to wander through life at our own choice and direction.

Paul is grateful to God that the Christians in Rome are clear-headed about this service of one master. By God's gift of grace, they have experienced the transfer of ownership from one slave-master to another. They used to be slaves to sin, but now they are slaves to righteousness: they have entered into a new life of joy and peace sustained by the power of God (verse 17).

There is some wonderful truth packed into the short sentence 'you wholeheartedly obeyed the form of teaching to which you were entrusted' (verse 17). Nowhere else in his writings does he use this deeply felt word 'wholeheartedly'. It conveys the idea of believers wanting to please their Master from the heart outwards. Obedience is a most important part of the Christian life and the sign of mature disciples (1:15; 15:18; 16:26) The word 'entrusted' pictures people being handed over from one owner to a new one. Now that we have left behind the old life of sin, our new master is Jesus. Christians are entrusted to his teaching, and this is like a mould that imparts its shape to our lives. (See Romans 15:1–6; Colossians 2:6–7; 1 Thessalonians 4:1–2; Titus 1:9.)

Throughout these verses, Paul is drawing the contrast between the two slaves-masters.

Sin as our slave-master

▶ Sin's slaves are in servitude. If we choose sin as our master, we can't help obeying the evil desires of sin (verses 12, 16).

▶ Sin's slaves get deeper and deeper into evil, described as 'impurity' and 'ever-increasing wickedness' (verse 19). Paul is perhaps thinking of patterns of human behaviour like those he described in 1:18–32.

▶ Sin's slaves feel shame. Obedience to this slave-master leads us to do things we deeply regret and blush to remember (verse 20).

▶ Sin's slaves are sentenced to hard labour. This is the sense behind the phrase, 'the wages of sin' (verse 23). The same wording was used for soldiers who received a pay-packet in the employment of the army; they earned their wages by the sweat of their brow, and received what they had earned.

▶ Sin's slaves die in service. The inevitable outcome of serving this slave-master is death (verses 16, 21, 23). If we reduce life to serving the body alone, death alone is the end. Sin promises life to the full, but it is a false hope, and at the end we receive what we deserve: death in all its forms, spiritual, physical and eternal.

God as our slave-master

▶ God's slaves are freed from the control of the old slave-master (verse 18). Liberty in Christ is an important theme for Paul, and he uses this terminology more than any other New Testament writer (8:2, 21; Galatians 5:1; 1 Corinthians 7:21–22). As we have seen, we are taught a pattern of teaching (verse 17) that moulds us into the liberty that belongs to the children of God (8:15).

▶ God's slaves can live a holy life (verses 18–19). As slaves to righteousness, we begin to see our characters transformed. As we offer the parts of our bodies in God's service, we discern the process of sanctification at work in us. Through the Holy Spirit's indwelling power, we experience increasing fruitfulness, reaping benefits (verse 22). Jesus promised this growing harvest of fruit to those servants whose lives are intimately joined to his (John 15: 2, 5, 8, 14, 16).

▶ God's slaves enjoy generous treatment. This slave-master does not pay wages, but he gives a free gift (verse 23). As in Jesus' parable in Matthew 20:1–15, God rewards us generously, even when we are not working. We receive in our salvation what we do not deserve. God does not pay wages, because he never owes us anything. This grace-gift is given to people utterly undeserving of it.

▶ God's slaves have the hope of life for ever (verse 23). The ultimate outcome of our sanctification is to share in the unending resurrection life of our Master (verse 22; 2 Corinthians 4:16 – 5:5).

Questions

1. What prevents or discourages us from practising this kind of obedience in our Christian life? What are the main obstacles – and how can we overcome them?
2. Is it right, or wrong, to go on feeling ashamed about sins in our past? Are there right and wrong sorts of shame? How can we deal with the wrong sort?

Romans 7:1-6

A story of two marriages

Death ends our obligations to the law and frees us to belong to Christ and serve him fruitfully.

We have seen that Christians live under grace and not under law, and are called to live as people who have been brought from death to life (6:12–14). We learnt  how the death of Christ changes our relationship to sin, so that we are no longer under its rule.

Chapter 7 expands what it means to live under grace. We shall see how Christ's death changes our relationship to the law, so that we are no longer under *its* rule. The section on 'Legalism' (p. 124) will help you to understand the passage.

Paul has both positive and negative things to say about the law. He restates the conviction he reiterates throughout the letter:

- the law can never be a way of salvation (3:20);

- the law is holy, righteous and good (7:13);

- the law is a way of discipleship for Christians, by faith in Christ and in the power of the Holy Spirit (8:4).

In the first section of chapter 7 (verses 1–6), Paul illustrates the difficult concept that our 'death' in Christ ends our obligation to the law's mastery.

You know the law

Paul assumes that his hearers will know what he is talking about concerning the law, and in particular that they will know that the law is binding on people only while they are alive (verse 1). He assumes this knowledge because his Jewish readers will have been brought up to know and honour the law, and Gentile converts would have been taught the Old Testament story from their early days as Christian disciples.

Here is an illustration

A married woman is legally bound to her husband. If she marries another man while her husband is alive, she clearly commits adultery. But if her husband dies, her marriage is legally over and she is free to marry again. No-one can disapprove of her actions on legal grounds. Death has ended her obligations to her previous husband and she is free to marry another man and take on obligations to him.

Verses 2–4 have prompted a variety of reactions. Some have found this marriage illustration confusing and unhelpful, because it fails the test of logic. They say this because in verses 2–3 it is the husband who dies (picturing the law) and in verse 4 it is believers who die (pictured by the wife).

Some use this illustration to support the view that once we become Christians we no longer have any obligation to laws and regulations, and the only 'law' we need to observe is the law of love. This incorrect use of these verses is supported by reference to 6:14 and 10:4. A complete study of all that Paul has to say about Christians' continuing relationship to the law, however, will demonstrate the false nature of this position.

The correct way to understand the marriage illustration of verses 2–3 is to use it not as an allegory (that is, applying every detail exactly), but as a picture of a central principle: death ends all obligations. Christians are like the wife. Before we become Christians we were under the power of the law. Through Christ's death the power of the law is ended. By faith in Christ we are freed to belong to him in a new, life-giving relationship.

Here is how the illustration applies

The married woman whose husband dies illustrates what has happened in Christians (verse 4). When Christ died on the cross, he took with him to the grave that old way of keeping rules and regulations in order to be right with God. Observing the law could never lead to salvation. But our union with Christ in his death on the cross radically alters our relationship to the law. God killed the effects of law, sin and death in Christ's body on the cross. Those who have put their faith in Christ can personalize the words of verse 4 and say, 'I have died to the law through the body of Christ in order to belong to another.'

Elsewhere Paul uses 'the body of Christ' to refer to the church (e.g. 1 Corinthians 12:27). However, this phrase in verse 4 refers to what Paul has said in 6:1–10 regarding Christ's body put to death and risen. When Christ died on the cross for us, he abolished in his body the law with its commandments and regulations (Ephesians 2:15).

These verses really tell a story of two marriages. There may be a suggestion in verse 4 that when we cease to be 'married ' to the law, we become 'married' to Christ. We then understand the reference to 'bearing fruit for God' (verse 4) as the fruit of the Spirit (Galatians 5:22–26), which may be likened to offspring born through our marriage to Christ. However, although Scripture speaks of God's people as a whole as the bride of God or Christ (see e.g. Isaiah 62:4–5; Jeremiah 3:14; Hosea 2:19–20; Ephesians 5:25–32; Revelation 21:9–10), it never applies this picture language to individual believers, and there is no mention of offspring.

The new relationship

Now that we are released from the power of the law, we enjoy a new relationship with Christ (verses 5–6). This is one of the Bible's 'what you were and what you are' passages. Previously, we were prisoners chained to a way of living described as being 'controlled by the sinful nature'. As we have seen from chapter 6, our bodies are not evil, but they are weak and open to temptation (6:13). We know from personal experience that laws that forbid and deny actually excite our curiosity and arouse a sinful desire within us to do the very things that are forbidden. Thus the law can actually provoke us to disobey (verse 5).

But now that we are Christians, united with Christ in his death on the cross, we have been released from this provocation to sin and set free to serve Christ. We are not free agents to do our own thing in the world; rather, we are liberated for a new kind of slavery – to Christ (Galatians 2:20). Paul draws a contrast between serving as slaves of Christ in the new way of the Spirit and our slavery to the old way of the written code (verse 6).

Note that this is not a contrast between law and Spirit, as if the law no longer matters, for the law still has a place in the Christian life (8:4). God has brought his Word and his Spirit together in our lives, as he promised through the prophet Ezekiel (36:26–27). The law of the Lord in Scripture is written on our hearts by the Holy Spirit. Because it reveals what kind of life pleases God, we are motivated, by our loving gratitude to him, to keep his laws through the indwelling power of the Holy Spirit. The new way of the Spirit (verse 6) is given the fullest interpretation in the teaching of Jesus in the Sermon on the Mount, and is introduced by the repeated phrase, 'You have heard that it was said ... but I tell you ...'. Read some examples of this new way of the Spirit in Matthew 5:21–26, 27–30, 43–48.

Forgiving: the old way and the new way

The contrast between the new way of the Spirit and the old way of the written code may be seen in a conversation between Jesus and Peter on the issue of forgiveness. When Peter asks Jesus if there is a limit to how many times he is expected to forgive his brother when he sins, and suggests the figure seven, he is thinking according to a written code of legal mathematics. In his reply, Jesus offers a new way of the Spirit for Peter to think about, and then tells him a memorable parable. He says to Peter: 'Stop counting, because forgiving someone is unlimited, unconditional and from the heart' (see Matthew 18:21–35).

Questions

1. How should we regard Old Testament law, according to this passage? What relevance to us does it have, if any? Why did Jewish Christians need to die to the law? Why couldn't they both obey the law *and* follow Christ as ways of salvation?
2. Think about 'bearing fruit for God' (verse 4). What is this fruit? Draw the tree of your life (birth at ground level) and mark on it the fruit you have borne or would like to bear in the future. Compare trees with others.
3. 'The new life of the Spirit' (verse 6). This is only the second reference to the Spirit in Romans (see 2:29). How does the Spirit tell us how to live our lives?

Legalism

Legalism is the belief that we can become holy and please God by obeying rules and regulations. The Christian life is seen as a list of do's and don'ts.

The weaknesses of legalism are that

▶ it fails to see the connection between law and grace;

▶ it does not understand the relationship between the law and the Holy Spirit;

▶ it concentrates on sins rather than sin as the root of the problem;

▶ it judges everything by external appearances rather than by inner disposition.

Read through Romans 7 – 8 and, with the following questions, try to gain a better understanding of legalism.
Why are legalists critical of other people?
Why is it difficult for legalists to admit to any error or fault?
Why are legalists often prone to a spirit of condemnation?

A further issue which cries out for attention is whether evangelicalism is a movement united around a few essential doctrines ... or by prescribed behaviour patterns. Is it any more than a religious subculture, held together by external and often restrictive codes of conduct? (Derek Tidball, *Who are the Evangelicals?* Marshall Pickering, 1994, p. 222).

Romans 7:7–13

Don't blame the rule-book

God's law is holy, righteous and good. In God's purposes it has a task to do in relation to sin, but this close relationship to sin does not make the law sinful.

After all that Paul has said regarding the law, he is bound to ask: is the law sin (verse 7)? He has hammered home the fact that conforming to God's law in order to gain merit with him is a false way of salvation. He has said some stark things concerning the law, and his comment that sinful passions aroused by the law are at work in our bodies (7:5) would have raised many questions.

Those who knew their Old Testament would be aware of passages in the Psalms that praise the value and blessing of the law: 'Great peace have those who love your law, and nothing can make them stumble' (Psalm 119:165); 'The law of the LORD is perfect, reviving the soul; the statutes of the LORD are trustworthy, making wise the simple' (Psalm 19:7).

Paul now has to defend the law. As God's gracious gift that defines what he requires from human beings, it is *holy*, *righteous* and *good* (verse 12):

▶ *holy*, in that it is set apart for God's purposes and reveals his character;

▶ *righteous*, or just, in that it fairly defines the terms on which we may have a relationship with the holy God;

▶ *good*, in that it has our well-being in mind and is intended to bring much blessing into our lives.

Paul makes three statements in his defence of the law.

The law shows us what sin is

If it were not for the law, we would not have any knowledge of sin (verse 7). This does not mean that someone who has never seen a copy of the Ten Commandments has no idea of sin. Paul has already explained in 2:14–15 and 5:12–14 that there is some inbuilt knowledge of God's laws in every human being.

Most cultures have a sense of what is right and wrong. Conscious experience of sin is not lacking. What Paul is saying is that God's law revealed to him the true nature of sin: that it is an offence against a holy God; that it consists in the ten offences forbidden by the Ten Commandments; that we are helpless under its power; and that we need someone to rescue us. James helps us to understand this use of the law by his illustration of the mirror. When we look into God's Word and read his law, if we are wise we will take good note of what we see, and do something about it (James 2:22–25). In the mirror of God's Word, the law can show us our need for a Saviour to rescue us from the power of sin and death.

As an example of the law's power to reveal sin, Paul chooses the sin of covetousness. The tenth commandment concentrates on inward desires, by contrast with the outward actions of the preceding ones. He probably chose this commandment because in his day it was seen as the cardinal sin from which all sins emanate. It was the sin that led to the downfall of Adam and Eve (Genesis 2–3). It was the tenth commandment that was the undoing of the rich young ruler who met Jesus (Luke 18:21). He was flawless in outward behaviour, but, when Jesus challenged him about his possessions, the law of coveting revealed the nature of sin in his heart.

The law provokes us to sin

From the days of Adam and Eve we have known the attraction of forbidden fruit. When we see a notice on a door that says PRIVATE – NO ENTRY, we want to disobey the command and see what lies behind it. Anyone who deals with young children will know how any command that forbids can provoke disobedience. This is what Paul means when he says that sin seized the opportunity afforded by the commandment (verse 8). In the Genesis story, the serpent was given the opportunity to strike with temptation only when God issued the command, 'You must not eat from the tree …' (Genesis 2:17).

Without a law to stir it into life, there is no sin. It is the law that gives sin its strength (1 Corinthians 15:56). Does this mean that the law itself is sin? By no means. Its function is to draw attention to the evil powers that are within all of us.

The language of verse 8 evokes a military operation: sin uses the law as a point of departure for war. Through knowledge of the law, sin can incite a rebellion, because we take pleasure in disobeying the rules. Without the law we would have nothing against which to rebel. Therefore, breaking the law makes rebels of us, and this rebellion reveals the true nature of our sinfulness. We choose to go our own way, and willingly exchange the truth of God for a lie and worship ourselves rather than the Creator (1:25).

The law leads to death

These three verses all refer to the law in relation to death:

▶ 'sin sprang to life and I died' (verse 9);

▶ 'the very commandment that was intended to bring life, actually brought death' (verse 10);

▶ 'sin ... deceived me, and through the commandment put me to death' (verse 11).

When he says that he was once alive apart from law (verse 9), Paul may be referring to his unity with Adam as the representative human being (5:12–21), of whom it could be said that before the fall, he was once alive apart from law. All others have been 'dead in ... transgressions and sins' from birth (Ephesians 2:1). Or perhaps he is thinking of his bar mitzvah ceremony when he was thirteen. In this ceremony a Jewish boy becomes 'a son of the commandment', and accepts responsibility to keep the law. From this age he is instructed in the law and taught to obey it.

The more Paul came to know the full requirements of the law, the greater became his knowledge of what God required. There was a time when he thought he was faultless with regard to the law (Philippians 3:6). But the risen Christ opened his spiritual eyes to see that all his good deeds were rubbish (Philippians 3:8). This destroyed any idea that he could be saved by keeping the rules, or that he was faultless and had led a blameless life. The true meaning of God's law came home to him, and on that day he died.

Paul had been taught as young man to learn and memorize the law. He was taught it in order to live it. Even though he had attempted to observe the commandments faithfully, and even though they were designed to bring life and blessing, he knew that he had failed to keep the law of God fully. Therefore he could say: 'the very commandment that was intended to bring life actually brought death' (verse 10). He now saw how sin had deceived him (verse 11) into thinking that if he did everything the law demanded, he would be acceptable to God. Sin deceived him into keeping the law for the wrong reasons. To follow the first commandment, and to love the Lord with all your heart, soul and strength, and your neighbour as yourself, would appear to bring great blessing. But this is the power of sin's deception. It deceives you into thinking that if you try hard enough, you can please God. You set about keeping a commandment you expect to be life-giving, and it actually brings about death.

In none of this is Paul suggesting that the law is at fault. The real cause of death is sin.

Questions

1. In many societies and cultures today, *wanting things* ('coveting') is *not* regarded as a sin. Why not? What is the effect of this on Christian families and churches?
2. In what ways do you think sin *deceives* us? (Note: Paul may have in mind the temptation story of Genesis 3:1–7.)
3. 'I died' (verse 9): Paul is thinking of being 'dead in … transgressions and sins' (Ephesians 2:1). How can we communicate to people what this kind of 'death' is, so that they may be attracted to seek life in Christ?

Who is the 'I' in Romans 7:7–25?

Who is Paul thinking of as he writes these verses? In verse 14 he changes from using the past tense to the present tense, and it is this autobiographical style that has posed the biggest problem for interpreting this passage.

▶ Is he referring to his state before he became a Christian?

▶ Or is he describing his experience as a born-again believer?

What lessons can we draw from this passage for either our pre- or post-conversion experience?

The evidence for each interpretation may be summarized as follows.

Paul is referring to his pre-conversion state

First, if Christians have died to sin and live a new life in Christ (6:22; 7:4), how can they be described as slaves to sin (7:14) and prisoners of sin (7:23)?

Secondly, there is no mention of Jesus Christ until verse 25, and no reference at all to the Holy Spirit. Yet the identifying mark of believers is the indwelling power of the Holy Spirit. It is impossible to imagine Christians, filled with the Holy Spirit, saying that there is no good living within them (verse 18). How can those who have been saved by faith in Christ cry out to be rescued because of their wretched situation (7:24)? This is clearly the language of unsaved people.

Thirdly, the fact that this comes before the teaching on life in the Spirit in chapter 8 suggests that Paul wants to show the stark contrast between the pre-conversion and post-conversion experiences. Following this argument, the latter part of verse 25 should be read as if it belonged earlier in the section, perhaps before verse 23. The first part of verse 25 then closes verses 14–24 with thanksgiving to Jesus Christ, who alone enables Christians to live victoriously as described in chapter 8. The problem with this approach is that there is no justification for moving the verses around in this manner.

Paul is describing his post-conversion experience

First, Paul deliberately changes from the past to the present tense for verses 14–25. Surely, if he was meaning to refer to his pre-conversion days, he would have stayed with the past tense.

Secondly, only a Christian could speak of law and sin in the way Paul does here: his hatred of sin (verse 15); his recognition that the law is good (verse 16); his desire to do what is good (verses 18–20); his delight in God's law (verse 20). Only Christians can cry out with thanksgiving for the victory they have experienced in Jesus Christ (verse 25).

Thirdly, the language of conflict in the Christian life is consistent with both Romans and the rest of the New Testament. Even when we know the joy of living the Christian life through the enabling power of the Holy Spirit, we still feel the tension between what we are and what we shall be (8:23). In fact, it is following Jesus that introduces us to a battle between the old, sinful nature and the new life of the Holy Spirit who indwells us (Galatians 5:17). We share in the victory of Christ's resurrection, but defeat and disappointment are not unknown in believers' experience. The early apostles would bear testimony to this disappointment from their own personal experience (Acts 15:36–41; Galatians 2:11–13).

Summary

In the study of verses 14–25 which now follows, I have followed the interpretation that Paul is describing the life of Christians *after* conversion. I will attempt to resolve some of the apparent contradictions as we go along.

It is important to read chapter 7 alongside chapter 8 and to see the intimate relationship between spiritual conflict in the Christian life and the Holy Spirit's help in dealing with this conflict. In chapters 7–8, Paul is not describing two stages of the Christian life. Rather, he is depicting two simultaneous aspects of it. Christians experience constant conflict between the old and the new natures, but the Holy Spirit enables us to live as God intended.

Romans 7:14-25

The constant conflict

Why is it that the good things which we know please God are the very things we find ourselves unable to do? Why instead do we become entangled with evil we know to be alien to our Christian character?

Remember to read chapter 7 in the context of what Paul has already said about Christians' status and, most importantly, what he will go on to say in chapter 8 on life through the Holy Spirit. Believers have to contend with constant spiritual conflict, but the Holy Spirit given to us delivers us from a state of impotence when we face temptation.

In these verses, Paul is not describing his daily experience of the Christian life. If he were, his use of words like 'wretched' (verse 24) might well leave us wondering about the truth of his mighty claims that the gospel truly sets us free in Christ. With emotional honesty, he is acknowledging those sad occasions when, acting out of character, we sin against what we know God's law requires of us as believers. These verses do not describe the experience of all Christians all the time. They do bear witness to what we all encounter some of the time. Paul is honestly asking the question all of us should face: why is it that as Christians we still have to contend with the power of sin in our lives? Surely we have been delivered from sin's control as our master (6:15-23)?

Spirit v. sin

We have already noted the change of tense in verse 14, from past to present. The most natural way to read these verses is to understand them as speaking about Paul's present experience as a believer (see 'Who is the "I" in Romans 7:7–25?', p. 129). He wants to address the conflict caused by the continuing presence of sin in Christians' lives.

'The law is spiritual.' This refers to its origin and authority. God gave us the law, and therefore it is trustworthy. Because it is spiritual, it has to be interpreted by those who are spiritually gifted. Believers have been granted the spiritual insight to understand that this spiritual law has exposed the true nature of sin in their lives; it has led them to put their faith in Christ, and they now know that it is by the power of the Holy Spirit that they can fulfil the requirements of God's law. The law was never designed to be a way of salvation, but it is intended to be a way of discipleship.

But the Holy Spirit has also revealed to Paul that he is unspiritual (verse 14). Although he is a born-again believer in Jesus Christ, he carries in his body a vulnerability to sin. At times, sin's influence feels so powerful that the only analogy he can draw is from the first-century world of slavery. He is sold as a slave to sin (verse 14). He feels as powerless as a slave who has been sold in the market-place and is led away with no control over his destination. This strong imagery, which at first sight seems wholly unsuitable to apply to those who are no longer under sin's mastery (6:17–18), is a sharp reminder that when we become Christians, sin does not just roll over and die. We may have been delivered from the mastery of both sin and death, but as Christians we are still subject to the influence of both these alien powers.

Paul v. Paul

This spiritual revelation leads Paul to suggest that he is a mystery to himself. He does not understand his own actions (verse 15). He knows the good he should be doing, but fails to perform it. He is genuinely perplexed that he does evil when he wants to do good, and even finds himself entangled with evil that his spiritual nature hates. It is no comfort that his intention to obey God's law indicates that it is good and attractive (verse 16).

The more he reflects on this constant conflict in believers, the more he perceives the continuing presence of sin. Sin has become like an unwelcome house guest, almost a squatter (verse 17). It has no right to be there, but Paul is helpless to evict the squatter and make sure it will never return. Paul is not passing the buck and suggesting that he is not responsible for his actions, but he is identifying the villain of the piece as indwelling and surviving sin (verse 20). This unwelcome house guest frustrates Paul's good intentions, making it impossible for him to put into practice the good things he would love to do (verse 18). What is worse, sin leads him into doing evil things. (Remember that Paul is talking of his life some of the time, not all the time.)

For Paul, this 'some of the time' experience would include the terrible falling-out with Barnabas (Acts 15:36–41), and his 'keep-fit' imagery of disciplining his body as a disciple of Jesus Christ (1 Corinthians 9:27). Passages such as James 4:1–12 (see also 1 Corinthians 6:1–11) remind us how a Christian congregation that loves and worships the Lord can also become entangled with sin. It is not too difficult to draw the conclusion that James sees the sins of individual believers in the church as a microcosm of the larger social sins of war, oppression and injustice.

Paul begins to summarize the law which he discerns is at work in him, that is, the law of sin. Here are six things he has learnt in his battle against it:

▶ He has an inward desire to do good, but realizes that evil is right alongside this good intention (verse 21).

▶ His true self as a believer delights in God's law, and who else but a believer could put it in these terms (verse 22)?

▶ As a believer, he is engaged in a battle for the mind, and the body is where sin makes its evil suggestions (verse 23).

▶ The wretchedness of this constant conflict causes deep frustration, a critical condition from which no human power can rescue him (verse 24).

▶ He gives thanks that God rescues him from this wretched state through Jesus Christ (verse 25).

▶ This rescue brings believers into a right relationship with God. But our new status as God's slaves does not deliver us from the continuing influence of sin (verse 25).

Questions

1. Are you surprised that Paul can write about himself in this way? Does this passage disturb or comfort you – or both?
2. Paul doesn't give specifics, but here we have the great apostle being very open about his moral failings. When should Christian leaders confess their sins publicly? And when should they not?
3. This passage has the quality of a hymn of confession, like Psalm 51 or Isaiah 59:9–15. Quietly compose your own hymn of confession, being as honest as Paul. Share it with others, if appropriate. If you need some inspiration, read 'Paul's wretchedness' below.

Paul's wretchedness

To press home the meaning of 7:14–25, look at Paul's heartfelt expression of wretchedness (verse 24), and link it with appropriate verses in chapter 8 on life in the Spirit. This will help you see how the Holy Spirit works through the constant conflict of the Christian life to produce in us wisdom, maturity and perseverance.

Here are seven examples of this approach:

1 When I am plagued by failure, I remember there is no condemnation for those who are in Christ Jesus (8:1).
2 When I am troubled about my thought life, I set my mind on what the Spirit desires (8:5).
3 When I wonder if God still loves me, I concentrate on the fact that the children of God are guided (8:14), confident (8:15), prayerful (8:15), assured (8:15) and spiritually wealthy (8:17).
4 When I worry about the ability of the universe to sustain itself, I remember that God is in control of his creation, and I seek to discern in his world the birth-pangs of a new heaven and new earth (8:18–23).
5 When I struggle with prayer, I work with the Holy Spirit, who helps me when words are difficult and my thoughts are confused (8:26–27).
6 When I cannot see how a sinful error of judgment can be undone, I believe that in all things God is working for the good of those who love him (8:28).
7 When I feel that the constant conflict with sin could endanger my relationship with the Lord, I am assured that nothing in the whole of creation can separate me from the love of God that is in Christ Jesus our Lord (8:35–39).

Look up each of these verses in chapter 8. Share in your group the insights you have gained about how the Holy Spirit helps us to live the Christian life.

LIFE IN THE SPIRIT

Romans 8:1–39

Stop and look

Chapter 8 is one of the great chapters of the Bible and has been called the Mount Everest of Romans. The chapter opens with 'no condemnation' (verse 1) and concludes with 'no separation' (verse 39). It concerns the invincible security of those who belong to Christ Jesus, and shows how the Holy Spirit works in believers helping us to overcome the inner forces of evil. The Spirit's work is the conspicuous new feature in this chapter, with nineteen references to him in the first twenty-seven verses. The chapter may be divided into four main sections:

▶ The Holy Spirit makes a new lifestyle possible (verses 1–12).

▶ The Holy Spirit assures us we are in God's family (verses 13–17).

▶ The Holy Spirit helps us in our frustrations (verses 18–27).

▶ The Holy Spirit affirms that God's love is invincible (verses 28–39).

Paul has said a lot about the weakness of the law to help us live the Christian life. The indwelling power of the Holy Spirit makes discipleship a possibility. Life in the Spirit is the birthright of every believer and the lifeblood of the church.

The Holy Spirit makes a new lifestyle possible

God has rescued us from an old lifestyle, and the indwelling power of the Holy Spirit enables us to live as he intended.

The heart of this passage is the conflict between walking by the Spirit and walking in the old, pre-Christian way (see Galatians 5:16). Paul has described the battle between our good and evil desires as a wretched experience calling for rescue (7:24) The opening word of chapter 8, 'Therefore', summarizes God's rescue plan for wretched strugglers. It is as if Paul is saying to himself, 'From chapter 3 onwards I have been sharing what God has done through the death and resurrection of Jesus Christ. On the basis of all that I have explained, I can confidently state that there is no need for those who are in Christ Jesus to be wretched and helpless.' He proceeds to give the details of this rescue plan.

Rescued from condemnation

Paul reminds us of the courtroom scene (3:24), where, instead of *our* being condemned for our sins and declared guilty, *Christ* is condemned for our sins (8:3) and we are acquitted. The word 'now' indicates that this gracious rescue from condemnation is something we experience immediately.

Later in the chapter we shall learn that the full blessings of God's rescue plan will involve complete redemption of our bodies. The presence of the Holy Spirit in us guarantees that this will happen (verses 23–25).

Rescued from helplessness

Because of the death and resurrection of Jesus Christ, we have received the gift of the Holy Spirit. His life-giving power is the indispensable mark of the true believer (verse 9). His presence in us does not make us instantly sinless, but he does deliver us from helplessness before the law of sin and death. We are liberated from the powerless feeling that comes from knowing the good we should be doing, and then giving in to evil desires (7:21). The Holy Spirit's powerful presence enables us to gain victory over sin now, and assures us of our ultimate victory over death (verse 11).

The price of this rescue from helplessness becomes clear as we read into the heart of verse 3. God sent his Son in the likeness of sinful human beings. Be careful: this does not imply that Jesus was sinful (2 Corinthians 5:21), nor does it suggest that his birth as a human being was less than real (only a 'likeness'). Jesus' body was sinless and real, and was nailed to the cross. It was in this supreme act of love that our sinful flesh was condemned. Therefore, there can be no condemnation for those in Christ Jesus, because he has already borne the condemnation we deserve (verse 3). The presence of the Holy Spirit in us means that what God commands, God enables us to do. There is no excuse for feeling helpless in the face of indwelling sin, as his plan for a righteous lifestyle becomes a real possibility by the indwelling power of the Holy Spirit (verse 4). (As a parallel to these verses, see Hebrews 2:14–18.)

Rescued from an old mindset

The way inner disposition controls outward lifestyle is an important theme in the Scriptures (see Jeremiah 31:33ff.; Ezekiel 36:26; Galatians 5:16–23), and Paul is about to offer two contrasting lifestyles with their corresponding outcomes. He describes these alternative lifestyles as 'living according to the sinful nature' and 'living in accordance with the Spirit' (verse 5). Each lifestyle has its control centre. One lifestyle is controlled by the sinful, self-centred nature (verse 8), and the other by the Spirit of God (verse 9).

It becomes abundantly clear that the only Christian lifestyle that pleases God and accords with what he intends is life in the power of the Spirit (verses 9–13).

It's obvious when someone is under the rule of the old, sinful mind.

The sinful mind reveals itself in behaviour. The works of the flesh, as listed in Galatians 5:19–21, include sexual sins and drunkenness, jealousy and discord. This is living according to the sinful mindset (verse 5).

The sinful mind is set on death. Not only is the mind invaded by a spirit of death, because it excludes any possibility of the life of God, but this lifestyle culminates in physical and spiritual death. There could not be a greater contrast with the mindset focused on God, which bestows a life of peace and total well-being, both now and in the life to come (verse 6).

The sinful mind is hostile towards God. This mindset is hostile to God and has no desire to do his will, nor is it able to keep his law. Therefore this lifestyle cannot please God (verse 8).

Rescued for new life in the Spirit

The Holy Spirit comes to do in us everything Christ has accomplished for us. His work is so essential that the Spirit's presence is the indispensable mark of believers. Without the Holy Spirit, no-one can claim to be a Christian (verse 9). Life in the Spirit is the normal Christian life.

He 'lives in you' (verse 9), indicating a settled, permanent presence, not an occasional visit. Paul uses different phrases to convey the same truth: 'those in Christ Jesus' (verse 1), 'the Spirit of God lives in you' (verse 9), 'have the Spirit of Christ' (verse 9), 'Christ is in you' (verse 10), all indicate the presence in us of the Father, the Son and the Holy Spirit. Someone has said: 'Wherever each is, there are the others also.'

Life in the Spirit does not mean that we become sinless Christians. Our human bodies are still subject to decay and death (2 Corinthians 4:16).

The difference for Spirit-filled believers is that our bodies are not ruled by sinful, self-centred desires (verse 10). Although still capable of moral and spiritual weakness, they are also the home of the Holy Spirit. He brings the power to live the Christian life as God intends it. His presence in us is a further sign that just as Jesus received a resurrection body after death, we shall know the Spirit's work after death, giving us new bodies for an eternal life that will not be subject to sin or decay (verse 11).

Questions

1. How can we experience the Holy Spirit as a settled, permanent presence in our lives and not as an occasional visitor? Be practical.
2. What are the things that shape your mindset? Imagine you are a visitor from Mars, conducting a sociological survey of the assumptions, expectations, convictions and fears ('mindset') of people in your society. What so you observe?
3. Romans 8:3 is a vital statement of the heart of the gospel. Rewrite it, expressing what it says *without* using the words 'law', 'sin', 'flesh' or 'offering'.

Romans 8:13–17

The Holy Spirit assures us we are in God's family

The Holy Spirit gives us resources to make us super-conquerors. One of these spiritual resources is membership in God's family. If we belong in the family, we should behave accordingly.

We enter God's family by a spiritual birth when God adopts us as his children. In these verses we are designated as either children or sons (including daughters). It is a specific work of the Holy Spirit to reproduce family characteristics which distinguish us as true children of God. Paul mentions five marks of the Holy Spirit's work of assuring believers of membership in the family of God.

We are guided into a holy lifestyle

When we are led by the Spirit we set our minds on what pleases God, and the Holy Spirit prompts us to reject ruthlessly what we know to be wrong. It is so ruthless it is described as a killing (verse 13). This is not a once-for-all killing. Jesus called his followers to take up their cross and follow him, and this is a daily discipline of discipleship (Mark 8:34). We cannot do this on our own, but we are given the Holy Spirit's power to help us. Being led by the Spirit is so important that Paul describes it as an obligation (verse 12), and faces us with a choice between life and death (verse 13). Ignore the Holy Spirit's leading, and continue to behave according to your old, pre-conversion life, and you will die. Be guided by the Spirit in putting to death the old lifestyle, and you will live. Look at Paul's practical guidance in Galatians 5:16–26.

We are confident

God does not expect his family members to exhibit a spirit of fear. He wants us to be joyful children, not frightened slaves (verse 15). The reference to slavery would strike a chord with readers in the first century, who well knew how slavery denied people their basic freedoms. (See the comments on 6:15–23.)

We have been set free from the slavery sin brings – especially slavery to fear of God as judge. Now, as newborn children, we have been introduced to our gracious heavenly Father and should revel in our freedom. Furthermore, God is delighted when his newborn children begin to call him by the family name (verse 15). The fear factor belongs to our old way of living. With the Holy Spirit living in us, we have to learn to be ruled by the faith factor, not the fear factor.

Timothy was a young pastor who was probably timid by nature in his dealings with members of his congregation. His older friend Paul gave him good advice when he encouraged him not to be a timid Christian. Rather, he should fan the fire of the Holy Spirit who was in him through the laying on of hands, and this would strengthen his courage (2 Timothy 1:6–7).

We are prayerful

When we talk to God in prayer, we reveal by the way we address him that we have not only the status but the heart of a child. *Abba* is an Aramaic expression meaning 'father'. Even today in some middle-eastern cultures you will hear children in the home using the word *Abba* when addressing their father. Jesus used this word when he was praying to his Father in the Garden of Gethsemane (Mark 14:36), and it probably began the Lord's Prayer in the Aramaic that Jesus would have used. We need to understand the radical newness of this word *Abba* on the lips of Jesus. The invitation to address God in the same trusting way a small child speaks to its father is startling.

Prayer is a 'heart and head' exercise. It is more than saying the right words; it is carrying in our hearts the disposition of children. This is why prayer has a special way of revealing to us our true status as God's children. We may not choose to use the word *Abba*, but we should discover patterns of praying which enable us to express the love and intimacy that God delights to hear his children express.

We have assurance

As we grow as believers, we learn to discern our own spirit telling us that we are children of God. We also discover that this inner voice of assurance is prompted by the Holy Spirit himself (verse 16). We say the words; the Holy Spirit supplies the witness. Paul would argue that since we have this double assurance of being children of God, there is all the more reason to live like his children.

We are heirs

The phrase 'heirs of God' (verse 17) occurs only here in the New Testament, and may refer to the children of God inheriting nothing less than the perfect life of God himself. The accompanying phrase 'co-heirs with Christ' is a sign that we are heirs only because of our relationship to him.

Since human heirs inherit the family fortune, our inheritance is a heavenly one which cannot be spoilt in any way (1 Peter 1:4). For God's children, the gifts and fruits of the Holy Spirit are the downpayment of our inheritance, guaranteeing that there is more to come (Romans 8:23).

Note that our inheritance is *conditional*. We must be prepared to share in the sufferings of Christ (verse 17). If we are willing to identify closely with Jesus in his terrible sufferings, we can expect to share with him in his glorious inheritance.

145

The Holy Spirit will teach us how to live with these great expectations.

Questions

1. How many different things is the Holy Spirit described as *doing* in this passage? Reflect on what each means for Christian living. Have you experienced each of them?
2. Think of some very young children you know, or of your own childhood. Who is it that influences little children most? Whose authority, ultimately, do they recognize? Meditate on the phrases 'led by the Spirit', 'spirit of sonship' and 'heirs of God' in this light.
3. Meditate on the last part of verse 17. Compare Acts 14:22 (in context). Why 'must' we suffer as God's heirs?

Romans 8:18–27

The Holy Spirit helps us in our frustrations

There are moans and groans in the Christian life. Moaning is futile. But the right kind of groaning can be filled with hope.

When we walk according to the Spirit, there will be difficult and painful times, but this is how we share in the sufferings of Christ.

The patriarch Jacob was tempted to think everything was against him (Genesis 42:36). There are times in the Christian life when we too face doubts and wonder what the Lord is doing to help us. When difficulties come, we often moan and groan. Moaning is futile. But this passage tell us that the right kind of groaning can be filled with hope. Paul describes three kinds of groan.

Creation groans

God intended human beings to manage his world under his direction (Genesis 1:28). When Adam and Eve disobeyed God's instructions and sinned, this was more than a personal matter between them and God. The whole creation suffered as a result of their fall. Disease, pain, death and environmental hazards entered God's perfect world. Read the prophet Joel's picture of an unhappy creation: 'The fields are ruined, the ground is dried up; the grain is destroyed ... and the fig-tree is withered' (Joel 1:10–12).

Paul has this same picture in mind of a groaning creation, and uses terms such as 'frustration' (verse 20), 'bondage to decay' (verse 21) and 'pains of childbirth' (verse 22).

This latter, poetic metaphor of birth indicates that the groanings will not last for ever. They are like the birth-pangs of a new heaven and new earth (Revelation 21:1). These groans will one day turn to glory (verse 18). The psalmist describes this joyful hope of a creation that anticipates liberation and freedom: 'let the rivers clap their hands, let the mountains sing together for joy' (Psalm 98:8).

Paul says the creation waits in eager expectation, standing on tiptoe with excitement (verse 19). What creation waits on tiptoe to see is believers openly recognized by the world as the sons of God. At present, those who believe and belong to Jesus Christ go incognito. One day we shall be revealed by God to be his true sons, and then creation will know that its own redemption is about to begin (verses 19–21).

Believers groan

This is not the despairing groan we utter when we are passing through hard times. It's the groan of feeling incomplete as Christians. When we accept the free gift of salvation in Jesus Christ, we are assured of its completeness, so we can truly say, 'I have been saved.' But while we are here on earth, we experience spiritual and moral weakness, and we long for the time when our redeemed bodies are set free from sin and frailty (verse 23).

This indicates that salvation in its complete sense is still to come. We feel incomplete because the physical redemption of the body lies in the future. We can certainly experience now what form of life awaits us then, because the Holy Spirit who lives within us is the firstfruit of the harvest to come (verse 23). The Spirit is also called the downpayment of our inheritance (Ephesians 1:14), guaranteeing that the remainder of the spiritual gift will be paid to our account later. Meanwhile, we are called to hope for this future event and wait patiently for it (verses 24–25), and we groan with longing for it to happen.

The Spirit groans

This groan expresses our weakness in prayer (verse 26). When we have those agonized longings for which we can never find the right words, God understands these prayers and the Holy Spirit does the praying for us (verse 26). There are prayers which are sighed rather than said, and in such moments the Spirit comes alongside to share in our weakness and put our painful thoughts into words that make sense to God. Such is the depth of this form of praying that in our dependence on the Holy Spirit we may be more in line with God's will than usual when we pray, because God knows us better than we know ourselves. He also knows perfectly the mind of the Spirit. Therefore he is able to hear and answer our prayers (verse 27).

A further truth is contained here. It may be that the Holy Spirit groans in believers' hearts because he is unable as yet to do his perfect work in us. James 4:5 and Hosea 11:8 may suggest that the Spirit loves us so dearly that he yearns for the day when we shall stand complete before our heavenly Father.

Questions

1. Groan 1: What sort of Christian 'ecology' does Paul teach here? How should we, as Christians, relate to the physical world around us?
2. Groan 2: Turn the 'groan' of verse 23 into a poem or song to express *your* longing for this 'redemption'.
3. Groan 3: Share experiences of this kind of praying. Do you think Paul could have speaking in tongues in mind?

Romans 8:28–39

The Holy Spirit affirms that God's love is invincible

God does not remove trials and difficult experiences, but uses them for our good. He has a plan for us and nothing can separate us from his invincible love.

 This magnificent section opens with a familiar verse (verse 28). God is always working for our good, so even the most difficult experiences may be seen to be part of his plan for us. Nothing that life can throw at us will ever separate us from his love (verse 39).

We have already seen how Paul uses the word 'waiting' (verses 19, 23). The Spirit can transform times of waiting into times of rejoicing. We are not in a tug-of-war contest, pondering the outcome of our Christian life. We know that the Holy Spirit, who is in us, is greater in power and wisdom than anyone or anything we may encounter in the world (1 John 4:4). There is a super-invincibility (verse 37) about the Christian life that is based on two principles.

God is following a process

God has planned that all true followers of Jesus Christ will become replicas of Jesus himself. God's design is to reproduce the image of the head of the family, Jesus (described here as the firstborn), in the rest of the family (verse 29). This is an amazing plan, which removes the emphasis from what we do as Christians to the work God is doing on our behalf.

Look at the way Paul describes this process (verse 30):

► Even before we were born, God had decided what he was going to do in us (*predestined*).

► He called us to follow him and then put us right with himself (*called* and *justified*).

► This work will not be finished until we arrive in heaven (*glorified*).

God is doing a work

Paul chooses to introduce us to the solid work God is accomplishing in our lives by asking four unanswerable questions: unanswerable in the sense that we can say nothing, but only affirm that God is invincible (verse 31).

If God is for us, who can be against us?

Our enemies in the Christian life can deflect us from our true goal of seeking first the kingdom of God (Matthew 6:33). The attractions of the world, the weakness of the flesh and the scheming opposition of the devil may appear to be an invincible trio. But the Holy Trinity is on our side. In all things God is working for the good of those who love him (verse 28); the Holy Spirit is helping us in our weakness (verse 26); and the risen and ascended Lord is praying for us (verse 34). This is no contest; your enemies may as well leave the battlefield!

Surely God will give us everything we need to complete our salvation?

God has given us Jesus as the most precious gift imaginable. If God has sent to earth his beloved Son and has not spared him the humiliation of the cross, we can be assured he will give us everything needful to complete our salvation (verse 32).

He died for us while we were sinners. If such a wonderful sacrifice happened before we became his children, there is no saying what God has in store now we are members of his family.

Can anyone bring a charge?

The third question brings us into a courtroom scene. Will anyone step forward as a witness to condemn believers? Is it possible that after we have repented and received forgiveness of sins, we could commit an unpardonable sin? Can anyone bring a 'guilty' charge against one of God's called and chosen children?

The devil will accuse us to our dying day (Zechariah 3:1; Revelation 12:10), but God will never take us to court again because Christ died for the very sins of which we are being accused, and on the basis of our faith in him we have been acquitted. His was a once-for-all death and we have received a once-for-all justification. When we do commit sin after we have become Christians, we still need to seek forgiveness and cleansing, and Jesus, as our advocate, speaks before God on our behalf (1 John 2:1). But we need never enter the courtroom again. That is guaranteed.

Can I be separated from the love of Christ?

The fourth question asks whether anyone or any situation could separate us from God's love (verses 35–36).

Paul describes some of those things that might threaten such a separation:

▶ the threats of a hostile, pagan society;

▶ the inevitable times of economic hardship; and

▶ the possibility of martyrdom for the faith.

Having concluded that we can be hyper-conquerors through the victorious power of the risen Lord who loves us (verse 37), Paul can imagine nothing, whether within or beyond our human experience, that can separate us from God's love (verses 38–39). Our God is invincible, and through our relationship with him we enjoy super-invincibility. That's the Spirit!

Questions

1. Think of a confusing or troubling time in your life. Can you see now how God was working for your good? What did you learn, or how did it change you?

2. In verse 36 Paul quotes Psalm 44:22. Read the whole psalm. It is the prayer of someone who felt that he *had* been cut off from God's power and love. Why does Paul quote this psalm?

3. Take each of the items in the list in verse 35 in turn, and illustrate it with stories of people who have faced these things victoriously in Christ. (Do a little research if necessary.) Why not put the result into a 'Romans 8:35 file' to encourage the rest of your church?

4. Review your study of Romans 1 – 8. What new things have you chiefly learnt?

GOD AND ISRAEL

Romans 9:1 – 11:36

Stop and look

At first glance it appears difficult to see how chapters 9 – 11 fit into the overall theme of Romans. Because they are rather puzzling, we are tempted to regard them as simply an interesting interlude in Paul's writing. They are like a half-time interval in a sports game. The first half is the gospel *explained*, in chapters 1 – 8; the second half is the gospel *applied*, in chapters 12 – 16. During the interval of chapters 9 – 11, are we listening to a talk by Paul on his home nation?

In truth, this section is an integral part of Romans and these chapters belong to the essential unity of the theme that has been unfolding from chapter 1.

One fact and three questions arise from reading chapters 9 – 11:

▶ God's chosen people have not believed his gospel.

▶ Does this suggest God's word has failed?

▶ How could this unbelief have happened?

▶ What implications does this have for the church of Jesus Christ?

There is absolute clarity in chapters 1 – 8 that the Jews were first in line to receive the gospel of God (1:16–17). There are constant references to the Old Testament Scriptures that promised this gospel to the Jews (1:2; 4:16). The Jews knew they were a privileged people who had been chosen and prepared by God (2:17–18). They were the custodians of God's amazing promises regarding the coming of Jesus as Messiah (9:4). But when the moment came and the promised Messiah appeared, the vast majority appeared to reject the gospel of God.

This apparent rejection causes Paul deep anguish of heart

(9:1). Has God's word failed (9:6)? How could it happen that the people of privilege did not welcome their Messiah? What caused the people of the Scriptures to be blind to the fulfilled promises staring them in the face? How was it that most of those who were destined to be the first in the queue for the gospel have turned and walked away? And what about the implications of all this for Christians? Chapter 8 ended on a high note of assurance. Nothing can separate us from the love of God in Christ Jesus our Lord (8:39). This strong confidence regarding believers' security in Jesus Christ poses a question that Paul must have been asked. How can God be trusted to be faithful to us, if it appears he has been unfaithful to Israel?

These are important questions, and Paul will take chapters 9 – 11 to address them.

▶ *In chapter 9 Paul defines the true Israel.* Israel has always been defined by God as a group within the nation and never the whole nation. The true Israel is not the whole of Israel.

▶ *In chapter 10 Paul explains the seriousness of Israel's disobedience to God's Word.* The counterpart of God's speaking is human responsibility to accept the truth of the gospel and call on the name of the Lord for his salvation.

▶ *In chapter 11 Paul expresses the hope of God's long-term plans for Israel.* Israel's present rejection will be reversed and will be seen to fit into God's overall purposes.

Paul has by now undertaken a number of missionary journeys, and, as the years have passed, the Jewish national rejection of the gospel has become more and more evident to him. Paul's intense sadness (9:1–3; 10:1) is the product of prayerful reflection on a truth that John's Gospel sets out: 'he came to his own home, and his own people received him not' (John 1:11, Revised Standard Version). As he contemplates his planned visit to Rome, he remembers the antagonism of the Jewish authorities in other cities and perhaps seeks to allay suspicion before he arrives. Acts 28 confirms this view.

Romans 9:1–13

God knows what he is doing

If nothing can separate us from God's love, why did God's chosen people reject Jesus when he came as the promised Messiah? Can God's promises be trusted?

What a change of mood as we move from the high point of the closing verses of chapter 8! Paul has revelled in our assurance as Christian believers and is convinced that nothing can separate us from God's love. He now reflects with a deep, intense sorrow at the plight of his own people, the Jews, and calls on the Holy Spirit, who has worked on his conscience, to witness to the serious spiritual situation of Israel's failing to recognize her promised Messiah (verses 1–2). Paul is responding to God as Moses did when he faced the unbelief of God's chosen people (Exodus 32:3–35).

So close are the family ties he feels with his people Israel that Paul was even willing to forfeit his own spiritual security in Christ if it meant that more Jewish people would come to place their faith in Jesus (verse 3). This disposition has much to teach us in our dealings with those who reject the gospel.

The privileges God gave Israel

In verses 4–5, Paul reminds his readers of eight privileges Israel enjoys by virtue of God's choosing them as his own people.

1 They were *adopted by God*. Out of all the nations of the world, God had adopted Israel as his own children, indicating a close personal relationship.
2 They were *given his glory*. He was with this one nation in a way he was not with any other group of people. The Shekinah cloud that followed Israel through the wilderness, and later dwelt in the Holy of Holies in the tabernacle, was a visible sign of God's presence among his people (Exodus 24:16–17; 40:34–38).
3 They *received special covenants*. God made covenant agreements with Noah (Genesis 9:9), Abraham (Genesis 17:2), Moses (Exodus 24:8), Joshua (Joshua 8:30ff.) and David (2 Samuel 23:5). God's covenant relationship with Israel is of fundamental importance. He committed himself to perform specific things for Israel, and in return obligations were expected of them.
4 They were *given the law*. God's gift of the law, and their continuing possession of it, constituted the Jews' greatest treasure. They knew that this was one of their highest privileges.
5 They were *given the temple worship*. Worship in the desert tabernacle prepared the Jews for the glorious worship that took place in the Jerusalem temple. A Jewish saying underlines how much these privileges meant to Israel: 'By three things is the world sustained: by the law, by the temple worship and by deeds of loving kindness.'
6 They were *given the promises*. Numerous promises of God are recorded in the Old Testament. While they were given first to Israel, which retains the privilege of having these promises in its literature, they are now open to the whole world. While all God's promises are important, Paul is probably referring to the ones about the gift of a Messiah.

7 They were *given godly leaders*. The patriarchs were the great founders of Israel's history. The term applies especially to Abraham, Isaac and Jacob, but is not limited to them.

8 They were *given the Messiah*. The patriarchs were part of Christ's human ancestry. God's plan for his Son Jesus was that he should be born and raised in a Jewish family, and through the generations he prepared a family line for this event. His divine son would be born of the virgin Mary. The opening of the New Testament reminds us of Jesus' human ancestors and his mother's obedience (Matthew 1:1–17). Here in this passage, Paul affirms Jesus' human ancestry as well as his deity (verse 5).

God's choice of Israel is challenged

In spite of these eight privileges, many in Israel failed to recognize the promised Messiah when he appeared on earth. He was rejected and crucified, and many of the Jewish people of the day colluded with the authorities in calling for his death.

Paul has to ask: does Israel's attitude mean that God's word has failed (verse 6)? Surely their rejection of Jesus is a massive blow to any claim that God's plans and promises cannot fail?

Paul now explains what the Bible understands by the term 'Israel', and provides a closer definition of precisely who has inherited these privileges (verse 6). The point to grasp is that not everyone in Israel was included in the covenant promise. God granted it only to specific individuals he chose. In the years that followed, Jews did not automatically inherit God's promises just because they were physically part of Israel. If they inherited the promises, it was because of God's free choice and their spiritual fidelity to God's word, not because of any natural advantages of birth or family inheritance.

Paul argues this point by reference to Abraham and his two sons, Ishmael (the elder son) and Isaac. Unusually in a culture that gave precedence to the firstborn son, God chose the younger brother and his descendants as the line from which the Messiah would come.

It is not that Ishmael was beyond God's mercy. In fact, God gives him special blessing (Genesis 17:20), and his descendants get a special mention (Genesis 36). But Isaac was the child God had promised (verse 8); he could not have been born without God's help, because Abraham and Sarah were too old to become parents. All this underlines that God's relationship with human beings is based on his grace, his choice and his mighty acts. Ishmael proves that natural advantages of parentage cannot inherit the promises. The fact that he had Abraham as his father did not qualify him as a child of promise (verse 8).

From verse 10, twin brothers, who had the same mother as well as father, are used to demonstrate that God's choice of people is not based on human merit or good character. (Paul is actually quoting Malachi 1:2–3 here, but you can read the whole story starting at Genesis 25:20.) God chose Jacob before he was born (verse 11). Before the character of either Jacob or Esau was evident, God had made his choice. Character and conduct are not the basis for God's choice. In fact, of the two men, Esau might well have been the more lovable character. But God had chosen Jacob to continue the line of the promise. This emphasizes the key gospel principle that we cannot be accepted by God on the basis of our good works.

The word 'hate' (verse 13) is a strong emotion to apply to a God who loves people (John 3:16). We should understand it in the light of Luke 24:26, where it indicates where love's priority lies. God loved both Esau and Jacob, but he loved Jacob more, and chose him and his descendants to bear his promises.

Questions

1. In verse 3 Paul prays like Moses in Exodus 32:31–32, after the Israelites had worshipped the golden calf. Should we follow his example? Under what circumstances?

2. In verse 11 Paul says that God distinguished Jacob from Esau 'in order that God's purpose in election might stand.' Why is God's 'purpose in election' important? How exactly does it work? Look back to Romans 8:28–30, and see also Ephesians 1:3–14.
3. 'Character and conduct are not the basis for God's choice' (see verse 11). Can you think of a real-life sketch to illustrate this? Do any of Jesus' parables illustrate it?

Romans 9:14–29

But God, that's unfair!

If God chooses some people and rejects others, is he unfair? Not on your life, says Paul. We need a deeper understanding of God's mercy and the sovereign way he works in history to achieve his loving purposes.

Paul has been showing that throughout the Old Testament period, God worked his purposes out through a small group within Israel, known as a 'remnant'. He  chose some people, such as Jacob, and rejected others, such as Esau (9:13).

Paul resorts to the diatribe style we have met before, in chapters 2 – 3. He creates an imaginary critic who raises questions for Paul to answer. The first question asks whether God is unjust to choose some people and reject others (9:14). Is God being unfair?

'Not on your life!' responds Paul. He begins his lengthy answer by quoting what God said to Moses, as recorded in Exodus 33:19, after the episode of the children of Israel and the golden calf. Israel did not deserve anything from God by virtue of their behaviour, but they received his mercy because it is in God's character to bestow compassion as he chooses (verse 15). The principle is clear: God's mercy has its source in his nature and cannot be influenced by our desire or effort (verse 16). The word 'effort' (literally 'running') calls to mind the vigorous exertion of athletes (it is used also in Philippians 2:16). However hard we try, we cannot influence God's choice. He has mercy on whoever he chooses.

Paul draws a further example of God's right to choose from the life of Pharaoh (verse 17). He was king of Egypt when God's servant Moses was calling for the children of Israel to be released from their slavery. Pharaoh stubbornly refused all Moses' pleas, and the Bible records that his heart was hardened. God had caused Pharaoh to appear on the stage of world history for two reasons: he wanted to display his power to Pharaoh, and he wanted the nations to know of his power to save (Exodus 9:16). The reference to God's saving power in the exodus deliverance should be linked to the saving power of God's gospel in 1:16. The nations did learn of God's saving power through the Israelites' encounter with Pharaoh (Joshua 2:10; 1 Samuel 4:8).

God chose to use Pharaoh in a negative way. As James Dunn puts it: 'Pharaoh was the darker melody in a minor key which played counterpoint to the major key of God's powerful call of Israel.' Pharaoh is typical of people who stubbornly resist God. Paul's readers with spiritual understanding would realize that this could be applied to those Jews who did not receive Jesus as the Messiah (John 1:11).

But was it fair of God to use Pharaoh in this way? Paul reaffirms the principle of God's right to choose and adds a further thought: God hardens those hearts he chooses to harden (verse 18). The hardening principle is again drawn from the life of Pharaoh, and there are numerous Scripture references to the hardening of his heart. Some passages speak of God hardening Pharaoh's heart (Exodus 9:12; 10:1); others say that Pharaoh hardened his own heart (7:13–14; 8:15). The most important feature of these verses is that God is never said to harden anyone who had not first hardened himself. There is always a period of patient waiting on God's part. God's mercy grants the hardened sinner an opportunity to repent (2:4).

But the questioner presses Paul again on the justice of God. Is it fair for God to blame us? We are surely helpless in the face of his power, if God can show mercy or harden us as he wills (verse 19).

Paul has four answers to this charge of unfairness.

Who are we to question God?

'O man' reminds us of the passage that contrasted Adam and Christ (5:12–21). Humans are made in the image of God and have a creaturely relationship with their Creator. This is not to deny the legitimacy of those questions that faith always asks. Paul is aware from the Old Testament that God is open to genuine questions of faith. Job asked God some challenging questions about personal suffering (Job 38 – 41); Jeremiah talked with the Lord about issues of justice because he could not understand why those who led sinful lives prospered (Jeremiah 12:1).

But this form of questioning in verse 20 arises from unbelief. God is our creator and we are the work of his hands. Can those who have been made ask their maker, 'Why did you make me like this?' (verse 20). The answer indicates that the question is unacceptable. Paul draws his conclusion from Isaiah 29:16 or 45:9–10, where the thought is God's creation of Israel.

God has the freedom of the potter

What right have we to challenge our Maker? Can you imagine a clay pot saying to the potter, 'Why did you make me like this?' (verse 20). Paul is drawing on familiar Old Testament passages in his use of the potter picture (Job 10:8–9; Isaiah 45:9–13; 64:8–9; Jeremiah 18:6–10). The potter has the right to use the clay as he chooses, and can refashion a flawed vessel on his wheel. He certainly doesn't need to explain to the clay what he is doing! Similarly, Paul suggests, God the divine potter is not answerable to those he has made. He has the right to make out of the same lump of clay a decorative vase for flowers and a functional pot for cooking. Whether the purposes are noble or common, the divine potter has the right to choose (verse 21).

Some object to this pottery imagery. They see it as unworthy and inappropriate. Human beings cannot be likened to clay pots. Clay is lifeless and passive in the potter's hand, whereas human beings have feelings, intellect and willpower, and a sense of justice that spurs them to protest to their Maker.

But God's choices are not capricious, nor does he exercise power over us for its own sake. When God does things we do not understand, and even when his purposes are not apparent to us, there is no reason to doubt that he is working out his just and loving designs (Romans 8:28). As James Edwards observes: 'Right is not right because God does it: rather, God does it because it is right. There is a moral order in the creation because there is a corresponding moral order in God.'

God acts in line with his character

We know from chapter 1 that God reveals his wrath and his mercy: his wrath to those who harden their hearts, and his mercy to those who trust him. Some read verses 22–23 as teaching God's 'double predestination' of the human race: God shows his wrath by bringing some sinners to destruction, and his mercy by bringing others to salvation. But read these verses closely. The vessels of wrath are 'prepared for destruction', but the vessels of mercy '*he* prepared in advance for glory'. God never prepares anyone for destruction; they prepare themselves by their own sin. God prepares people for glory. Sinners prepare themselves for judgment.

Notice that God 'bore with great patience the objects of his wrath' (verse 22), and read more about the purpose of God's patience in 2:4 and 11:32. Look again at the life of

Pharaoh and reflect on God's patience with him in the light of 2 Peter 3:9.

God foretold these things in the Old Testament

Pharaoh's hardening of heart led to the exodus from Egypt. Israel's hardening of heart led to the revelation of God's love in Christ Jesus, which has resulted in riches for the whole world (verse 23). This includes the Gentiles. People some Jews may have regarded as 'pots for common use' had been chosen by the potter to display his glory. Through the ministry of Paul and other missionaries, great numbers of Gentiles were turning to Christ. Quoting from Old Testament passages, Paul proves that God had always intended from the beginning to bless Gentiles as well as Jews.

The quotations from Hosea 2:23 and 1:10 are taken as prophecies of the staggering inclusion of those who were not God's people, the Gentiles (verses 25–26).

The quotations from Isaiah 10:22–23 and 1:9 foretold that only a 'remnant' of believing Jews would remain. Even this remnant is a miracle. But for the intervention of God's grace, Israel would have been destroyed like Sodom and Gomorrah (verses 27–29).

Chapter 9 began by asking: 'How can we explain the unbelief of Israel?' The answer has been that God knows what he is doing. The whole Old Testament story bears witness that what he does is consistent with his character, and with his 'word' and promise to Israel. As John Stott observes: 'It is because he is who he is that he does what he does.'

Questions

1. How does the story of Pharaoh help us to understand what Paul means by 'hardening'? What are the signs of 'hardening'? Is there no cure?
2. How much of our lives is the creation of the Potter? And how much is our responsibility?

3. In verses 19–20 Paul is drawing on the story of Job, although at first sight Job certainly does 'talk back' to God in complaint about his sufferings. But in the end God *commended* Job for the way he spoke (Job 42:7). How does Job illustrate what Paul has in mind?

Romans 9:30 – 10:13

Human responsibility

Israel is responsible for her own plight. She has made wrong choices, with serious consequences.

 The greater part of chapter 9 has been about God's choosing people, what Paul terms 'God's purpose in election' (verse 11). The verses in this passage show how Israel chose wrong ways of trying to be right with God:

▶ a wrong direction of living – it was the way of works (9:30–33);

▶ a wrong kind of zeal – it lacked knowledge (10:1–4);

▶ a wrong way of thinking – it forgot the way of faith (10:5–13).

And God holds Israel responsible for these wrong choices.

There is a tension between the facts that God chooses people (election) and that people choose for themselves (human freedom). Earlier in chapter 9 Paul has been explaining why we are saved (verses 6–29) – because God chose us. The verses we are now studying explain why people are lost – because they chose wrongly. The two themes are not contradictory; they complement each other. Charles Spurgeon, a great preacher of the nineteenth century, commented on this apparent tension between divine election and human freedom: 'I never attempt to reconcile friends.'

A wrong direction of living

Paul describes the reversed situation of Gentiles and Jews (verses 30–31):

▶ Gentiles have gained what they were not seeking – the way of being right with God based on faith.

▶ Israel was zealously seeking a way of being right with God, but they failed to attain it because they were pursuing the way of works.

Israel is humanly responsible for her wrong direction of living, says Paul. First, she *misunderstood the purpose of the law*. Instead of allowing the privileges of the faith (9:1–5) to lead her by the hand of faith to Christ, she had perverted their purpose and made them a substitute for faith in Christ. God's gift of the law was intended to show us our need of Christ and his willingness to save us (7:13). But Israel thought that by keeping the law she could please God, and that he was obliged to recognize her good deeds and reward her (3:20).

Secondly, Israel *stumbled over the stone*. God's 'stone' is a major theme of the Old Testament which is taken up by the New Testament writers. The 'stone' is Jesus. His life, death and resurrection are a strong foundation on which we may build our lives. Either we build on this rock, or we stub our toes on it. If we refuse Jesus as the foundation stone, he becomes the stone over which we stumble.

Paul uses the stumbling-stone theme elsewhere to illustrate that the cross of Christ can trip people up in their thinking (1 Corinthians 1:23); Peter quotes the 'stone' passages in his letter (1 Peter 2:6–8); and Jesus takes the reference to the 'stone' from Psalm 118:22 and applies it to his own ministry, with a devastating picture of what happens when people refuse to build their lives on God's stone (Matthew 21:42–44).

Paul quotes Isaiah 8:14 and 28:16 to highlight the positive and negative results of the stone. Ignore the stone that God has provided, and you will stumble and fall; receive by faith the gift of this stone and build your life on Jesus Christ, and you will never look back or be ashamed of this wise choice (verse 33).

A wrong kind of zeal

Paul knew from personal experience that it was possible to 'stumble over the stone' and ignore the true significance of Jesus Christ. But from the bottom of his heart he was praying that what had happened to him on the Damascus road would also occur to many in his nation (10:1).

He further analyses why Israel has not seen in Christ Jesus a foundation stone for being right with God. He knows they have a religious zeal, but it is misplaced and lacks knowledge (verse 2). He recognized it from his pre-conversion days; it had led him to reject Christ and persecute the church (Galatians 1:14; Philippians 3:5–6). He can now clearly testify that he has turned his back on those days when misguided zeal ruled his life (Acts 26: 9–18).

Israel's wrong kind of zeal places her in a serious situation. They do not know or submit to the righteousness that comes as a gift from God. Rather, they have tried to establish their own way of being right with God. Their zeal in following their own way of religion has blinded them to the truth that Christ's coming has put an end to law-keeping as a way of being right with God (verses 3–4).

A wrong way of thinking

In pursuing this theme of Israel's responsibility, Paul

167

contrasts the way of law-keeping and the way of faith. Israel has submitted to a wrong way of thinking and has chosen to try to be right with God by law-keeping. This is in spite of the Old Testament Scriptures that speak of the way of faith. He reminds his readers of some basic Old Testament facts about the way of faith.

Obey the whole law and you can be right with God

Moses had stated that you can be right with God by keeping the law, but only if you kept it perfectly (Leviticus 18:5). Again, Paul knew of this way of thinking from his pre-conversion days, when he saw himself as blameless in keeping the law (Philippians 3:6). He now realized that he was blameless only in the sense that he appeared so to other people. But he was not blameless in God's eyes, and no-one could ever claim to have kept the law perfectly. No-one (3:9–20)!

The way of faith is easily accessible

The quotations from Deuteronomy 30:12–14 originally referred to the nearness of the law, but Paul applies them to Christ Jesus. We do not have to go spiritual mountain-climbing or deep-sea diving to discover God's way of faith. It is easily accessible to us in Jesus. He was born among us; that is, he has already been sent from heaven as the Messiah (verse 6); he was raised from the grave and appeared to his disciples after his resurrection (verse 7; John 20:20).

Faith is believing and confessing

The quotation in verse 11, from Isaiah 28:16, reminds us that the basis of faith is not doing something but trusting someone. It is as old as Abraham, and those Jews who knew their faith should have remembered this principle (Romans 4). Faith believes in the heart that God raised Jesus from the dead. Faith then confesses with the mouth that Jesus is Lord (verse 9). This is the earliest confession of faith and was probably used by candidates in open-air baptismal services. 'Heart and mouth' faith in Jesus Christ is the basis for being right with God. Being right with God by faith means we are justified and saved (verse 10).

This way of faith is freely available to everyone

The next verse Paul quotes from the Old Testament is Joel 2:32, which reminds Jews and Gentiles that God has no favourites (verses 12–13). This way of faith is open to everyone without distinction. Paul has already emphasized that there is no difference as regards sinning; all have sinned and come short of God's glory (3:23). Equally, there is no difference as regards being saved; all who call on the name of the Lord will be saved (10:13).

Do not miss the reference to the rich blessings salvation brings (10:12). Read Jesus' parable in Matthew 20:1–16 to understand the riches of God's grace.

Questions

1. Do you think Christians can fall into these same three traps (wrong direction, wrong zeal, wrong thinking)? Can you illustrate how we could make the same mistakes?
2. How does the parable of the prodigal son (Luke 15:11–32) illustrate Romans 10:1–4?
3. Paul may be quoting a baptismal confession in 10:9. Have a go at rewriting the whole passage, to turn it into a kind of baptismal confession for yourself. (For instance, starting with 9:30: 'I was not looking for God and a way of being right with him, but …)

Romans 10:14–21

God's mission plan for the world

Israel can never claim she did not hear the gospel or understand God's purposes in Jesus Christ. The problem is not sufficient knowledge but obstinate unbelief.

These verses deal with God's mission plan for the world. If people are saved when they call on the name of the Lord (verse 13), how do they come to call in 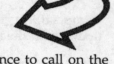 the first place? Was Israel given a fair chance to call on the Lord's name?

Paul addresses this in four rhetorical questions (verses 14–15):

▶ How can people call out to be saved without faith in the one who offers salvation?

▶ How can they put their faith in someone they've never heard of?

▶ How can they hear unless someone tells them?

▶ How can people share the gospel message unless God commissions them?

The first thing that has to happen before people can call on the Lord, then, is that messengers have to be sent to tell them about him. The gospel is not a human initiative; it is God's message, and he calls and equips his messengers.

Secondly, those messengers have to proclaim the message so that people 'hear' it – so that they get the full picture and understand it.

Thirdly, the hearers need to believe the message and

place their faith in the one who offers them salvation.

Finally, believing that the Lord can save them, they can call on his name.

These verses are often used to spur us into evangelism today. While this is entirely valid, we should remember that Paul is asking whether the *Jews* had heard and understood the gospel. Insufficient numbers of them have been calling on Jesus Christ for salvation (verse 16). This failure to believe was foretold by the prophet Isaiah (53:1). So what went wrong? Haven't they heard? Didn't they understand?

Haven't they heard?

Any possibility of excusing the Jews on the ground that they hadn't heard (verse 18) is swept away by the quotation from Psalm 19. This psalm shows that God has revealed himself in the world (verses 1–6) and in his Word (verses 7–11). Paul has in mind the first part of the psalm, which speaks of God's glory revealed in creation. Although this revelation is universal, Paul is not claiming that every individual has heard this good news. (Remember that one of his purposes in writing to the Romans was to establish a mission base for taking the gospel to unevangelized Spain.) He probably means that after twenty years of mission outreach through the early church, there must be very few synagogues whose members have not heard the story of Jesus of Nazareth, who claimed to be the promised Messiah.

From the beginning of Jesus' ministry, preaching the gospel to the Jews had a been a priority. He had proclaimed it widely in the synagogues. He had sent the twelve disciples out on mission with the instruction that they were not to go among the Gentiles, but rather to the lost sheep of Israel (Matthew 10:5–6). In the days after Pentecost, the church's preaching was initially directed to Jewish people and Gentile converts to the Jewish faith (Acts 3:12–26; 8:26–40).

So there could be no excuse on the ground of insufficient opportunity to hear the gospel.

Didn't they understand?

Even if they had heard the gospel, perhaps they could be excused on the grounds that they found it difficult to understand (verse 19). Paul combines two Old Testament passages to refute this excuse. Deuteronomy 32:21 is a reminder that even Gentiles have understood the gospel. Some of the Gentiles who turned to Christ in faith would have had Philistine, Samaritan and Babylonian ancestors. Jews would regard people such as these as ignorant in matters of faith, and as nations of nobodies (verse 19). Isaiah 65:1 builds on this theme (verse 20). The Gentiles did not seek God in the way the Jews did, but nevertheless they found him because God reveals himself even to those who are not seeking him. It wasn't that the Jews didn't understand. Rather, they didn't *want* to believe. God has constantly stretched out his arms of welcome and friendship to Israel, but has been met with disobedience and obstinate rejection (Isaiah 65:2, quoted in verse 20).

In chapter 11 we shall discover that God's grace has an answer for disobedience and obstinate rejection. The story of Israel is not over yet!

Questions

1. Do you have to be specially appointed to be an 'evangelist', before you can spread the gospel? This seems to be what Paul says in verse 15. What is the 'sending' he has in mind?
2. Does anyone in today's world have an excuse because they have not heard? Who? Why? What is needed? (Some research using Patrick Johnstone's Operation World would help here.)
3. There are four quotations from Isaiah in this passage, one from Deuteronomy, and one from the Psalms – a selection from the twenty-nine Old Testament quotations in Romans 9 – 11, all made from memory. What should we learn from this?

Evangelism

Every disciple is called to be a witness to Jesus and to be involved in evangelism (John 20:21; Acts 1:8). Some Christians have a special gift that enables them to communicate the gospel with especial relevance and clarity.

One of the best-known definitions of evangelism is by Archbishop William Temple: 'To evangelize is so to present Jesus Christ, in the power of the Holy Spirit, that men and women shall come to put their trust in God through him, accept him as their Saviour, and serve him as their King in the fellowship of the church'.

The word 'evangelism' means the announcement of good news. God has given us a message about the life, teaching, death and resurrection of Jesus Christ to share with other people (John 3:16; Romans 5:8). If people are going to believe this good news, they must be given every opportunity to hear it in a language and form they can understand (Romans 10:14–15). While the message never varies, the methods we use will differ from culture to culture.

Read Corinthians 9:19–23 for an insight into Paul's evangelistic methodology. Look at verse 22, and give examples from your own experience of what it means to become all things to all people, so that by all possible means we might see people saved by Christ.

Romans 11:1–10

A partial rejection

God has invested too much in Israel to reject her. He has chosen a small, faithful minority to achieve his purposes. But he will harden the hearts of those who wilfully reject his love.

The theme of chapter 11 is clearly stated in verse 2: 'God did not reject his people, whom he foreknew.' Everything we have read in chapters 9 – 10 would  appear to indicate that he *had* rejected them. Israel had received every opportunity to hear the gospel, but had forfeited these blessings through unbelief and disobedience (10:21). Surely, they had lost the opportunity to be God's people who received the promises.

Such a conclusion reckons without God's grace. Paul states emphatically that God has not rejected his people Israel, and presents his evidence.

A remnant is chosen

First, Paul invites us to consider his own conversion (verse 1). Paul was a 'class one' Israelite (see Philippians 3:4–6). Would he have become a Christian if God had given up on Jewish people? He was not an ordinary Israelite; he had been a blasphemer and fierce persecutor of the church, and yet God had called and chosen him (see Acts 9:1–2).

Secondly, Paul cites the story of Elijah in 1 Kings 19 (verses 2–4). Elijah thought all Israel had forsaken God. In a dramatic incident, God told him that seven thousand people remained faithful to him, albeit unknown to Elijah. The faithful seven thousand were the 'seed' or 'remnant' in which lay Israel's hope. God was keeping faith alive in the nation through a faithful remnant. This is still his method of working.

The 'remnant' were those who remained faithful because of God's grace, not by their own merits. There was probably a large remnant of believing Jews in Jerusalem in Paul's day (see Acts 21:20). God had chosen them in his grace; it did not depend on the character or qualifications of individuals. In his great love, God takes the initiative and chooses people to be his messengers.

Others are hardened

To explain why Israel as a whole has not recognized Christ as Messiah, Paul speaks again about the hardening of hearts (verses 7–8). We have met this before in Romans: when people refuse to believe God's way of salvation, he gives them up to the corrupt desires of their hearts (1:18–32; 9:18).

Using Deuteronomy 4; Isaiah 29:10 and Psalm 69:22–23, Paul illustrates how God gives people up to their stubbornness to believe. When people refuse to look for him and listen to his words, God makes their vision dim and gives them deaf ears (verse 8). His laws and promises should be like a joyful feast. But sadly, persistence in unbelief turns a table of good food into a snare (verse 9).

God can make us walk tall in his world with that clear-sighted wisdom that comes by knowing Jesus Christ as Saviour and Lord. But when people reject God's offer of good news, they are destined to spiritual blindness (verse 10). God never intended it to be this way, but he has hardened their hearts, underlining the truth that God does set limits to people's wilful unbelief.

Questions

1. Do you think Jewish Christians today could say the same as Paul in verses 1–2? Find out as much as you can about 'messianic Jews', and pray for them.
2. A difficult (but very important) question: why does Paul

175

picture God as the giver of the blind eyes and deaf ears in verse 8, when it is people who are responsible for the rejection of the gospel?
3. Think about the story of Elijah, from which Paul draws encouragement in verses 2–5 (1 Kings 17 – 18). Do you find Elijah's story encouraging in your circumstances at the moment?

Romans 11:11–24

A temporary rejection

Israel's rejection of the gospel is temporary. God uses their unbelief as a means to save the Gentiles and achieve his ultimate purposes for the Jews.

The opening verses of this chapter concern the Jewish 'remnant chosen by grace' (verse 5). But what of the majority of Israel, who were hardened (verse 7)?
Have they stumbled beyond recovery (verse 11)? Have they forfeited their chance to believe? Paul replies with another decisive negative: 'Not at all!' The rejection by the majority of Israel is temporary, and has a part to play in God's plan of salvation for the world.

Paul changes the tone of his approach in these verses, and now directs his warning to Gentiles (verses 20–21). Interestingly, for the first time in chapters 9 – 11 there are no direct quotations from the Old Testament, though the illustration of the olive tree is probably drawn from Isaiah 56:3–8. To explain the purpose of this temporary rejection by Israel, Paul paints a series of pictures.

The conversions that provoke envy (verse 11). Jewish

communities persistently refused the gospel of Jesus Christ brought by Paul on his missionary journeys (see Acts 13:46; 28:28). So Paul and his colleagues turned to the Gentiles, who responded in faith and obedience (Acts 14:27). This had the effect of awakening unbelieving Jews to a realization of what they were missing, and aroused their envy (Acts 5:17; 17:5).

The loss that leads to gain (verse 12). The mystery deepens as we observe the fruitful connection between the Jews' saying 'no' to the gospel and the Gentiles' saying 'yes'. The Jews reject a blessing and the Gentiles receive it. What is more, if the Gentiles gain spiritual wealth when the Jews stumble over the true identity of Jesus as the Messiah, what kind of wealth might the world receive when the Jews accept the gospel and are spiritually resurrected (verse 15)?

The preaching to one group that benefits others (verses 13–14). Paul begins to speak to the Gentiles in personal terms and explains the purpose of his ministry. He has already explained God's order for preaching the gospel: first to the Jews and then to the Gentiles (1:16). Because of the Jews' unbelief, this order is now reversed, so that Gentiles precede Jews. But Paul remains convinced of God's plan to heal the breach between Jews and Gentiles and make one new community in Christ. It is important, therefore, to continue to include the Jews in God's plan as outlined in 1:16.

Paul knows that God called him to be an apostle to the Gentiles (verse 13). His best chance of winning the Jews is by reaching the Gentiles. This arouses the Jews' envy, but the goal is to see some of them saved (verse 14). In this way, he believes, the commission to preach the gospel to Jews and Gentiles is being fulfilled.

The rejection that promotes reconciliation (verse 15). Paul's use of the word 'reconciliation' indicates that he is thinking of the death of Christ (5:10–11; Colossians 1:20–22). Through Christ we have received reconciliation: through his death, Jews and Gentiles have been reconciled to God in one body. This is a wonderful work of grace, and the number of Gentile believers confirms this miracle. The spiritual miracle yet to come is Israel's acceptance of Christ, and this will be like a resurrection from the dead. Some see this verse as referring to the resurrection of the dead that will precede the return of Christ (Matthew 24:30–35).

The firstfruits that signal a greater harvest (verse 16). Here is further evidence of the temporary nature of Israel's rejection. The image is taken from Numbers 15:17–21, where the dedication of the firstfruits is a sign that the whole belongs to God. So when the first converts believe, it is a sign of more to follow. The present small number of Jewish converts are the firstfruits of Israel as a whole. Greater numbers of Jewish Christians are anticipated.

The tree that receives new branches (verses 17–24). Paul's parable of the olive tree may not make horticultural sense to us (some suggest that Paul as a city-dweller was confused in his use of the imagery). The interpretation hinges on the phrase 'contrary to nature' (verse 24).

In fact, the grafting of wild olive shoots into an ailing olive tree was a normal procedure in Paul's day. It had two results. The ingrafted shoot was able to bear olives, and the ailing tree was given new vigour. Therefore Paul is correct in his use of the parable, and the phrase 'contrary to nature' refers to the unnatural belonging, not the unnatural grafting, of the wild shoot. 'God is not bound by the limits of what people see as natural' (Leon Morris).

The parable pictures Israel as a cultivated olive tree. Unbelieving Jews are branches of this tree which have been broken off because of their unbelief. Believing Gentiles are like a wild olive shoot grafted in and nourished by the cultivated root. But they have not displaced the branches that were broken off. God has not discarded these branches; they can be grafted back into the tree again (verse 23).

God has only one tree. The root of this tree, which gives life to the branches, both Jewish and Gentile, is the story of salvation from Abraham to Christ (2:28–29; 4:22–25).

The parable is designed to achieve two things.

First, it warns Gentile believers not to boast (verse 18) and not to display arrogance, but to live in the holy fear of God (verse 20). They must not look down on the Jews as broken branches. The same could happen to them if they were to allow their faith to degenerate into arrogant presumption (verse 21). They could suffer the same fate as the Jews and be cut off by the sternness of God (verse 22).

Secondly, the parable promises restoration for the Jews. If God can take the wild olive shoot of the Gentiles and graft it into the tree of salvation he had been cultivating since Abraham, 'how much more' will he be able to take the old branches (unbelieving Jews) and graft them back into their own olive tree, where they naturally belong (verse 24)? This hope deepens Paul's conviction that Israel's rejection of the gospel is temporary.

Questions

1. What does the passage say to us (Gentile Christians) about our attitude towards Jews and Judaism?
2. How do you think Paul 'made much of' his ministry (see verse 13)? Why did he do this? Should we do something similar? Why, and how?
3. Is it realistic, today, to think of Jews being made 'jealous' and so prompted into faith in Christ? How might this actually happen in practice?

Romans 11:25–36

A purposeful rejection

God has revealed something previously hidden, and is proved to be wise in his dealings with Israel.

From the beginning of chapter 9 Paul has been addressing the thorny problem of why the Jewish nation has not acknowledged Christ as the Messiah. He now comes to his principal answer, which he terms 'this mystery' (verse 25).

The mystery is revealed

We normally use the word 'mystery' to indicate something that can be known only to the initiated. In this context Paul uses the word 'mystery' to mean something that was previously hidden but has now been revealed by God. (It also occurs in 1 Corinthians 2:7; 15:51; Ephesians 3:4.) The revealed mystery is to be openly proclaimed among those who are in God's family. Paul is particularly concerned that Gentile Christians should not be ignorant of this mystery. He has challenged them about their tendencies to pride and conceit (verses 18, 20, 25). He must have met Gentile believers who looked down on the Jews, perhaps thinking that God had finished with them because of their unbelief. If these Gentiles are shown the meaning of the mystery, it will stop them being conceited (verse 25).

In verses 25–27 Paul explains this mystery. Part of Israel has become hardened against the gospel by unbelief. But this is a temporary situation until the completion of the missionary task among the Gentiles. When the full number of Gentiles are converted, all Israel will be saved. Paul supports his reasoning by scriptures from the Old Testament.

The question arises: what does Paul mean when he says that 'all Israel will be saved' (verse 26)? Does 'all Israel' mean:

▶ spiritual Israel – Jewish and Gentiles believers together?

▶ every single Jew without exception?

▶ or the vast majority of Jews, but not all individuals?

Does 'saved' mean:

▶ saved by faith in Christ?

▶ or saved on the basis of the original covenant with Abraham?

The only way to approach these questions is in the context of the parable of the olive tree (verses 17–24). The Jewish branches have been broken off the tree of salvation because of their unbelief (verse 20). But if the Jewish branches do not persist in unbelief (verse 23), and turn in repentance and faith to Jesus Christ, they will be grafted back into their own olive tree where they belong.

The statement that all Israel will be saved must indicate a large number of Jews, but in the context of all that Paul has said in this letter, their salvation must be through faith in Jesus Christ. The Old Testament passages quoted in verses 26–27 confirm this. The salvation will be accomplished by the deliverer from Zion (see Isaiah 59:20–21; 27:9). This refers to the first advent of Christ, who came to turn Israel from godlessness and to lead them to repentance (verse 26), and to implement his covenant, which provides forgiveness of sins (verse 27).

The enemies are loved

The mystery continues to unfold as Paul describes the

consequences of Jewish unbelief. They are enemies in all senses of the word (verse 28): enemies of God because of their unbelief, and enemies of the Gentiles out of envy (verse 11). But the amazing heart of this mystery is that the door that shuts out Jewish unbelievers is the door that opens to believing Gentiles. The phrase 'enemies on your account' means that the Gentiles have spiritually prospered through the Jews' unbelief (verse 12).

But the enemies, the unbelieving Jews, are still greatly loved by God on account of his promises to Abraham and the patriarchs (verse 28). God cannot forget his covenant love towards Israel, because his gifts and calling are irrevocable (verse 29), and he has not given up on his special people.

The disobedient find mercy

God is not defeated by human disobedience.

▶ There are disobedient Gentiles who are not in God's family (verse 30).

▶ There are disobedient Jews who reject Jesus Christ (verse 31).

▶ There are Gentiles who receive mercy and are admitted to God's family (verse 30).

▶ There are also Jews who receive mercy, and they are re-admitted to God's family (verse 31).

God in his mercy knows that the hardening and unbelief of Israel are necessary steps on the road to her salvation. This is the only way she will be rid of her self-reliance. Paul considers that the disobedience of unbelief that hardens the heart is like an imprisonment, and only God's mercy can release the prisoners (verse 32).

To God be the glory!

What a hymn to conclude the chapter! In his four-verse doxology (verses 33–36), Paul praises God's mystery and majesty. Although it is a worthy conclusion to chapters 9 – 11, the apostle probably has in his mind the long journey from 1:16 as he composes this hymn, drawing on rich Old Testament passages.

Paul does not claim to have all the answers. He may have explained God's mystery, but there is still much that is hidden. Paul did not necessarily see all the practical details of how this serious situation of unbelieving Israel would be resolved. But this hymn reveals that he was content to leave its outworking to God's mercy and wisdom.

Praise God's wisdom!

Who would have guessed that God would turn Israel's disobedience into salvation for the world, and then employ the Gentiles' obedience to reverse Israel's unbelief? This is deep wisdom, immeasurable and incalculable. There is no way that we can fathom this kind of wisdom. God is far beyond us, and our minds cannot comprehend his greatness. We cannot keep track of such a God, because his paths cannot be traced. The 'depth of the riches' means that 'salvation is a gift from God's riches and it immensely enriches those to whom it is given' (John Stott).

Praise God's power!

The hymn asks three questions, to which the answer is always 'No'.

- Has anyone ever been able to anticipate what God is going to do?
- Has God ever needed anyone's advice?
- Has God ever been short of resources and in need of a loan?

The very ideas are absurd. (See the passages Paul quotes: Isaiah 40:13; Job 41:11; 1 Chronicles 24:14.)

Praise God's majesty!

God's supreme majesty and self-sufficiency mean that everything in the universe depends on him:

▶ He is the Creator – 'from him'.

▶ He is the Sustainer – 'through him'.

▶ He is the Goal – 'for him'.

And so with Paul we sing: 'To him be the glory for ever! Amen.'

Questions

1. Do you think that Paul has in mind a *process* (Jews being converted through 'jealousy') or an *event* (a mass conversion of Jews in the future)?
2. Make a list (in discussion if possible) of God's 'paths past tracing out' (verse 33). What are the questions you would love to know the answers to? Try to turn each question into an expression of *praise*, as Paul does here.
3. Look back over Romans 9 – 11. What is the chief impact it has made on you? Has your view of God changed? Has your attitude towards the Jews been affected? Has your understanding of the Old Testament been deepened?

BELIEVING AND BEHAVING

Romans 12:1 – 13:14

In chapter 12 Paul begins to unpack the implications of living the Christian life. Chapters 1 – 11 have dealt mainly with matters of doctrine and belief. Some ethical issues were dealt with in 6:12; 7:6 and 8:9, but Paul now offers detailed practical guidance for everyday living. This section through to chapter 16 demonstrates that doctrine and duty belong together. A right relationship to God has been the theme undergirding chapters 1 – 11; right relationships with people will characterize chapters 12 – 16. This new way of relating to people is of fundamental importance, because God has widened the membership of his family to form a multiracial church of Jews and Gentiles (15:8–9).

This connection between believing and behaving has close resemblances to the teaching of Jesus (John 13:17), and the parallels between these chapters and the Sermon on the Mount should be noted. (Compare 12:14 with Luke 6:28; and 12:17 with Matthew 5:39. Compare 12:20 with Luke 6:27.)

The shape of chapter 12 bears out this relationship between believing and behaving:

▶ Because you have received God's mercy, offer your bodies (verses 1–2).

▶ Because you are in Christ's body, serve one another (verses 3–8).

▶ Because you must leave room for God's judgment, don't take revenge (verses 9–21).

In view of God's mercy, Paul appeals to his readers to behave in line with their beliefs. When we offer our bodies, and our minds are transformed, we can know and do God's will.

 These verses set the direction of the next five chapters. Having demonstrated the depth and wideness of God's mercy in chapters 1 – 11, Paul now urges us to respond in two ways: by offering God our bodies and by being transformed in our minds.

Offering our bodies

'Therefore' refers to all that Paul has said so far about God's mercies. This has been a central motif in the preceding chapters (e.g. 9:23; 11:30; 11:32), and Paul now grounds his urgent appeal in this theme.

The call to 'offer your bodies' is couched in the language of sacrifice, which would be familiar to Paul's first-century readers. The old order of sacrifice in the Old Testament involved the death of animals. The new way of sacrifice for Christians is the daily offering of a life of service in the world (Hebrews 13:15; 1 Peter 2:5). Under the old order the sacrificial gift, once offered on the altar, belonged no longer to the worshipper but to God. We have been purchased with a price, Christ's sacrifice; we are no longer our own persons (see 1 Corinthians 6:19–20), but are to offer ourselves wholly to God for his service. We are to present our bodies because it is in our bodies that we live the Christian life.

Paul has already spoken about this. He has warned us

not to offer the parts of our bodies to sin, as 'instruments of wickedness' (6:13), and encouraged us to present them 'in slavery to righteousness, leading to holiness' (6:19). This suggests the total offering to God of the whole body, not just in the cloistered places such as church services, but in the down-to-earth living of the Christian life in every conceivable situation. Animals were killed on the altar, but ours is a living sacrifice: we offer God a dynamic, vital Christian life, full of spiritual promise, for his service in the world.

Such an offering is a 'spiritual act of worship'. This phrase can be translated in various ways: 'the worship of God by mind and heart'; 'our logical and reasonable service'; 'an act of intelligent worship'.

The strength of 'spiritual act of worship' is that it heightens the contrast between the ceremonial and the spiritual. In the ritual of worship, there is always a danger that worshippers might honour God outwardly while their hearts are not loving God or seeking to serve his kingdom (Matthew 15:8–9). By contrast, spiritual worship involves mind and heart. We must be thoughtful and spiritual worshippers, and think through what it means to offer the Lord 'our logical and reasonable service'. Christian sacrifice is not a matter of the lip alone, but also of the life.

Being transformed in our minds

If we are the ones who are to offer our bodies, God is the one who transforms us by renewing our minds. These verses explain the process of sanctification. It is God's work, by his Spirit, to make us like his Son.

First, we are warned not to conform to the pattern of this world (or age). In the memorable paraphrase of J. B. Phillips, 'Don't let the world around you squeeze you into its own mould, but let God remould your minds from within.'

Paul, writing his first letter to the church at Corinth, warns these believers about conforming to the philosophers (1:20), wisdom and rulers (2:6) and standards of this age

(3:18). Jesus warned his disciples not to be squeezed into the religious patterns that belong to this age. His watchword for nonconformity was 'Do not be like them' (Matthew 6:8). We no longer live for this age alone. We live in this age, but we belong to the age to come (Ephesians 1:21; Romans 8:23–24). For believers, the old has gone and the new has arrived (2 Corinthians 5:17).

Secondly, this negative warning is followed by a positive command: 'be transformed'. This is transformation at the deepest level, the continual process of renewal of the mind. God does this as we study his Word with others and are open to the promptings of his Holy Spirit. He teaches us God's good, pleasing and perfect will, and thus transforms our minds.

There are links between the words 'transformation' and 'transfiguration', and it is helpful to read Mark 9:2–8 (the transfiguration of Christ) and 2 Corinthians 3:18 (the transformation of Christians). To paraphrase Mark 9:2, 'a complete change came over Jesus'. The complete change that comes over believers is nothing less than the work of God, who reshapes our character and conduct to make us like Christ Jesus.

Why does God undertake this task of transforming Christians' lives? Because he wants us to test and approve his will. We learn what God wants us to do, and in the power of the Holy Spirit we set to work to do it.

Questions

1. Why do you think Paul lays emphasis on the 'mind' here, rather than on the 'heart'? Look back to Romans 8:5–8 in thinking about this.
2. Personal spiritual audit: review your thought-life. Write down ways in which your thought-life is still 'conformed to this world' and needs to be 'transformed'. Share your list with others if appropriate, and set yourself goals for change.
3. Bodies come in all ages, shapes and conditions, wrapped

in clothes, attached to families (or not), and laden with possessions (or not). How can we make the offering of our bodies real, in worship?

Romans 12:3–8

Self-appraisal

Christians belong not only to Christ, but to every member of his body. God gives us gifts for the benefit of the whole body, and each of us needs to discover the nature and purpose of our gifts.

Paul is writing to Christians who are members of diverse congregations in Rome: diverse in race, culture, and social and religious background. His task is to teach these believers how to relate to other Christians, Jewish and Gentile, and to highlight their new corporate identity as the community Christ has called into being.

We know from our readings in Romans that some Jewish members tended to boast of their national heritage as the chosen people (2:17), while some Gentile believers behaved in a superior manner towards their Jewish brothers and sisters (11:18, 25). On all sides there was a danger of too much self-esteem and too little dependence on one another. With this background in mind, see how Paul addresses the congregations.

Honest self-appraisal

A priority for all members of a Christian community is an honest appraisal of their own gifts. The word 'think' (verse 3) reminds us of the encouragement to be 'transformed by the renewing of your minds', and honest self-knowledge is an early sign of the fruitfulness of God's work of grace in our lives. Thinking with 'sober judgment' means thinking with good sense and clear vision, appreciating that every Christian has been given a gift by God and has a responsibility to understand his or her gift and its purpose in the body of Christ. Paul's message is not just for those who imagine themselves to be gifted; he speaks 'to every one of you' (verse 3).

A sober estimate will not only help us to realize the gifts we possess, but will encourage gratitude towards the Giver. This is the meaning of the phrase 'the measure of faith God has given you' (verse 3). All of us depend on the Giver, so there can be no room for boasting, pride or superiority.

The one body has many members

The image of the church as a human body with diverse members is common in Paul's writings (see 1 Corinthians 12:12–20; Ephesians 4:4–16). Just as a human body has many parts with different functions, so the church has many members with different gifts. Paul emphasizes that the body is united in Christ. This is what holds this diverse membership together. Moreover, we are more than members of the same body. Each of us belongs to all the others. There is no room for private faith or isolated discipleship. It could not be plainer: if we are related to Christ, we are related to one another.

The whole congregation is equipped with gifts

All of us who are members of Christ's body have received grace gifts. The various lists of gifts in the New Testament (1 Corinthians 12 – 14 ; Ephesians 4:11–12) are not meant to be exhaustive. God has given today's church gifts that edify the body of Christ but are not mentioned in these lists. Paul's point is that the life of the Christian community depends on God and his grace gifts. Every church is a charismatic community, for without God's gifts of grace (*charismata* in Greek), we could not function as the church of Jesus Christ.

The phrase 'according to the grace given us' underlines that we cannot claim credit for either the natural abilities we possessed before conversion or the spiritual endowments given to us at conversion. Everything we have is God's gracious gift to us.

The gifts are diverse

Paul lists seven gifts in verses 6–8, five of which are of a practical, caring nature.

Prophecy

This gift was highly esteemed in the early church and is the only one to be mentioned in every New Testament list of gifts. With the apostles, prophets are mentioned as the foundation of the church (Ephesians 2:20). Prophets were gifted to speak words of guidance to the church. Read Acts 11:28–30 and 21:10–11 to see the gift of prophecy in action, and 1 Corinthians 14 for a fuller treatment of its role in the church. The latter part of verse 6, 'use it in proportion to his faith', may be better translated 'use it in agreement with the [Christian] faith' as a whole (see the NIV marginal note). This underlines the Bible's emphasis on the dangers of false prophets and the need always to weigh and test a prophet's words (1 Corinthians 12:3; 14:29; 1 John 4:1–6).

Serving

This word is linked to all the gifts, but has particular reference to those men and women who serve as deacons (the Greek word often translated 'deacon' is the word for 'servant'). There are numerous Bible references to the exercise of this gift of service, and Jesus in his ministry set the pattern for all our serving (Mark 10:42–45; Acts 6:1; 1 Corinthians 12:5). Although even our speaking ministries are to be exercised in a spirit of service (2 Corinthians 5:18–20), the routine and mundane business of operating the life of the church requires a grace gift if it is to be effective.

Teaching

Ever since his friend Barnabas brought him to Antioch as a Bible teacher for young converts (Acts 11:25–26), Paul had excelled as a teacher of the whole counsel of God (Acts 20:27). More than anyone, he knew the value of this gift. Teachers were gifted to explain the Old Testament, share the stories of Jesus' life and pass on his words. The early church did not have libraries of books to consult, and many of its members were unable to read or write, so the young congregations were heavily dependent on this gift of teaching.

Encouraging

The ministry of encouragement is a powerful gift to any congregation, and Barnabas is often cited as the supreme New Testament example of this gift in action (Acts 4:36; 9:26; 11:23). Note the links between this gift and the consoling ministry of the Holy Spirit, described in John 14:16–17; 15:26.

Sharing, leading and caring

These functions are grouped together at the end of this list and show the character of people God has gifted rather than being the gifts themselves.

▶ If you have the gift of sharing with others, your giving will be generous.

▶ If you are gifted as a leader, your leadership should be diligent and zealous.

▶ If your gift is caring for the needy, do so with cheerfulness and joy.

193

Questions

1. Do you think Paul just has individual, local churches in mind, or is he thinking more broadly? How might his teaching about 'grace gifts' apply *between* churches, in regions, or to the universal church of Christ?

2. In assessing our own 'grace gifts', our judgment can be distorted either by self-importance (the problem Paul mentions, verse 3), or by its opposite, an excessively low self-image. How can we overcome both, and achieve 'sober judgment' about ourselves?

3. Personal spiritual audit: in pairs with someone you know well, write down what you think are *your* 'grace gifts' for the church of Jesus Christ, and what you think are the gifts of the other person. Then compare and discuss the results.

Spiritual gifts

The main passages on spiritual gifts are Romans 12:6–8; 1 Corinthians 12:4–11, 28–30; Ephesians 4:7–13 and 1 Peter 4:10–11. They do not add up to a complete catalogue of the gifts God gives his church, but list examples.

In 1 Corinthians 12 Paul explains the spiritual gifts and their purpose:

▶ They are *spiritual* (verse 1). We may have natural gifts of music, management or hospitality, but we need God's power to make them into gifts that build up the church.

▶ They are *gifts* (verse 4), given out of God's generosity. They are not rewards for good behaviour or medals for faithful service.

► They are intended for *service* (verse 5). Jesus' whole life was an act of service (Mark 10:45), and our gifts should be used in the same way: not as spiritual toys for our own pleasure, but as spiritual abilities to build up the church (see Ephesians 4:12–13).

► They are a sign of God *working* (verse 6). When a Bible passage is made plain, God is at work. When a congregation is encouraged by an act of generosity, God is at work. When someone is healed, God is at work.

► They are manifestations of the Spirit's diversity (verses 7, 11). The gift of knowledge reveals God's truth. The gift of mercy reveals his compassion. The gift of evangelism reveals his love for his enemies. All this is for the 'common good' of the local church (verse 7).

1 Corinthians 13 reminds us that *love* is the controlling factor when using our gifts.

Romans 12:9–21

Love makes the difference

Love is the hallmark of the church and of our witness to the world. God gives us the supernatural ability to reveal his love in all our relationships.

Paul has already written about God's love for us (5:5, 8; 8:35, 39). Now we are to learn that the gifted church (12:3–8) can function only if love pervades its whole life. Our transformed minds (12:1–2) can understand that the love of Christ, which has been poured into our hearts, now has to flow out to others: first, to the church family (12:9–13), and then to the wider community of a sometimes hostile world (12:14–21).

Love is the centrepiece of this passage. Love defines the nature of the church. 1 Corinthians 13 reminds us that the work and witness of the most gifted Christian community imaginable could be rendered null and void if love were not controlling the exercise of the gifts.

In the first section (verses 9–13), Paul shows how love *acts*. In the second (verses 14–21), he shows how love *reacts*.

How love acts

Love is genuine (verse 9). Love must be sincere, that is, without hypocrisy. Behind the Greek word for 'hypocrisy' is the idea of an actor who wears a mask to disguise his true appearance. It is important for our life together in the church and our witness in the world that our love should be without masks. Love lacks sincerity when it wears a mask of sentimentality to make light of wrongdoing, or a mask of manipulative behaviour to get what we want, or a mask of pretending to love people when deep down our feelings are entirely the opposite.

Love is good (verse 9). Closely allied to love's sincerity is its hatred of evil and its cherishing of the good (verse 9). We face a choice between good and bad courses of action every day. The mind that is being transformed (12:2) will cultivate a deep hatred for evil and a firm attachment to the good that triumphs over evil (verse 21).

Love is affectionate (verse 10). Both the terms used here are family words. Paul's word translated 'devoted' is the love of parents for their children, and 'brotherly love' is the deep affection of siblings for one another. We know from our personal observation of both family and congregational life that normal affectionate relationships are not a universal experience. But the ideal of love in the church calls us to treat our co-members as our brothers and sisters in Christ.

Love is humble (verse 10). Love can honour others for their gifts and rejoice when they are given greater honour within the community. We are to consider our sisters and brothers better than ourselves (Philippians 2:3).

Love is eager to serve (verse 11). Love never lacks zeal for the Lord's work. It is never lazy, but always fervent. The same phrase is used of the gifted Apollos, who spoke with great fervour (Acts 18:25). The ardent love that comes from the Spirit should propel us into steady, consistent service for the Lord. The church needs members committed to serving the Lord, come wind, come weather, and who faithfully keep their promise. When serving the Lord becomes wearisome, we remember that Jesus offers to refresh those who are hard-pressed and burdened (Matthew 11:28–30).

Love is joyful in hope (verse 12). The early Christians had plenty of reasons not to hope, as they faced the world's hostility. But they knew that an integral part of their corporate witness was to rejoice in the Lord, even when they were unable to rejoice in their circumstances (Philippians 4:4). We learnt from chapter 5 that hope gives Christians the long view on life and opens the door to joy.

Love is patient in affliction (verse 12). The word 'affliction' indicates that believers may face serious trouble. They need to show steadfast courage under pressure. Once again the teaching of Romans 5 is relevant to this verse. The Bible clearly teaches that we must expect to face trials of faith (2 Corinthians 4:7–12, 16–18; James 1:2; 1 Peter 1:6–7), but love can triumph in the face of tragedy.

Love is faithful in prayer (verse 12). Prayer requires persistent faith and spiritual endurance (Luke 18:1; Ephesians 6:18), and God's grace enables us to grow in this spiritual discipline.

Love is generous to needy people (verse 13). They are not to be marginalized and treated as second-class citizens (James 2:14). The situation James describes is not so far from our experience today. We must work to make our church fellowship aware of the needs in and around it, and find ways of meeting them.

Love is hospitable (verse 13). Rome was a mecca for merchants and visitors from all over the world. The Roman congregations were under pressure to offer hospitality to large numbers of people. This of course included Paul, who later indicates that he would like to stay in the city for a period of time (15:24). The early congregations did not have their own buildings where they could house visitors, nor was it safe or desirable for travellers to use the local inns. Paul is aware that for the church in Rome, of all places, a huge resource of sacrificial love was required to meet the need for hospitality. (See also 1 Timothy 3:2; Titus 1:8; Hebrews 13:20.)

How love reacts

Verses 14–21 address Christians who might be going through the fire of persecution The congregations in Rome, Antioch and other major cities would feel vulnerable in the face of a largely hostile world that did not understand this new sect called 'Christians' (Acts 11:27). Paul offers practical advice on loving attitudes and a loving lifestyle. We are to love our opponents in such a way that the gospel of God is commended.

Verse 17 may be used as guide to the rest of these verses:

'Do not repay anyone evil for evil. Be careful to do what is right in the eyes of everybody.' Similar passages confirm that Jesus' teaching about overcoming evil with good had permeated the life of the early church: Matthew 5:39; Luke 6:28; 1 Corinthians 4:12–13; 1 Thessalonians 5:15; 1 Peter 3:9.

Love fights evil with good. When a congregation comes under attack, their response may well surprise their opponents. They are advised not to curse, but to bless (verse 14); not to retaliate with an evil action when evil is done to them (verse 17); not to take revenge, but to leave room for God's judgment to work (verse 19); and not to use evil methods to fight evil, but to use loving deeds to turn enemies into friends (verse 21). They must even offer hospitality to their enemies (verse 20). The phrase 'heap burning coals on his head' is picture language for making your enemy burn with shame. When enemies realize they are on the receiving end of so much love from those they have maltreated for being Christians, they may turn and repent.

Love is sensitive to others' feelings. The congregations in Rome are to be so immersed in the life of their community that they know the houses where there are joy and laughter and those where there are tears and sadness, and respond appropriately (verse 15). They must willingly associate with people of lower social status (verse 16). As they live in harmony with one another – each one different, but each contributing to the symphony of their corporate life – they will commend the gospel to those outside.

Questions

1. In your group (if possible), share testimonies about 'heaping burning coals' on someone's head (verse 20). How does it work in practice – and how can we generate the love and patience to do it?
2. Paul's picture of 'love without masks' is very attractive. But what do we do when things go wrong, the masks go

back on, offence is given or taken, and love and zeal die away? How do we put things right?

3. If your group is creative, try to turn this passage into a drama or mime; or write 'A day in the life of Soon Ho Lee, our hopeful Chinese friend', illustrating his struggle to live out the Christian life.

Romans 13:1–7

Christians and the state

Christians are citizens of two kingdoms: God's eternal kingdom and an earthly state. How can we behave in our earthly societies according to the values of God's kingdom?

Paul's opening words about submission to the government (verse 1) don't necessarily relate to *any* kind of regime that might be in power. He has in mind a settled and ordered situation where the state is fulfilling God's divine purposes. The important issue of relating to evil or tyrannical regimes is not considered here. Just as God's divine purposes for the institution of the family stand, even though individual families may fail to reach the ideal (Ephesians 5:22 – 6:4), and the sinful behaviour of members of a congregation does not negate the divine institution of the church (1 Corinthians 5), so Paul in this chapter is unfolding the proper function of the state as intended by God, without getting into a discussion about specific abuses and shortcomings.

Other passages deal with evil governments as strong-holds of Satan and how believers should respond to state persecution (Revelation 13; 12:11). Paul could have drawn on his considerable experience as a travelling missionary who had suffered physical abuse administered by representatives of the state (Acts 16:22–23; 24:23–27). The early Christians knew there were occasions when the state overreached its powers, and Christians then had to obey God rather than ungodly rulers (Acts 4:19). Bearing this caution in mind, we can now turn to Paul's wise teaching on the purpose of the state.

Christianity started out with a tremendous handicap in the eyes of Roman law because its founder, Jesus, was executed by the sentence of a Roman governor. This meant that from the outset, Christians had to be particularly careful of their public behaviour. Christians will be all the more effective in their witness, and enjoy easier and happier relations with the state, if they show willingness to co-operate with what the state legitimately demands.

Paul says four things about government according to God's purposes in these verses.

Its divine origin

Every Christian is to submit to the authorities, because God instituted them. No particular kind of government is commended. All systems are included – imperial, monarchical and republican. This does not mean that all the powers accord with God's will in what they do. There are good and bad authorities, God-fearing and godless governments. But state authority as such is instituted by God. Ordered government is not a human invention. It is part of God's created order and provision for the well-being of societies.

Its protecting role

Believers must respect the powers of the state because God intends the governing authorities to maintain a safe and peaceful environment where sin and evil are restrained and citizens can build their lives in caring and creative communities. Where there is safety and liberty, the church also is able to flourish and grow.

Terrorists may think they are fighting a human system, but Christians know better. Terrorist rebellion against a government is rebellion against God and incurs judgment. Whether they realize it or not, the incumbents of the Kremlin, the White House and 10 Downing Street all fulfil their functions under the judgment and mercy of God.

But there is an important qualification. The word 'obey' is not used in this chapter. There are certain things that the government has no right to order. Jesus makes this clear in reply to a question about paying taxes to Rome (Luke 20:22–25). Coins that bear Caesar's image belong to him. But God puts his image on people, and they belong to *him*. Therefore governments cannot demand worship, nor may they forbid the worship of God (see Acts 4:19–20; 5:29). There is no justification for using this passage to support uncritical submission to unjust, evil, atheistic regimes. Human rights and religious liberty are the heritage of every Christian community, and those of us who live in free societies should always be vigilant in raising our voices on behalf those who are persecuted for their faith.

Its authority under God

The authorities have a duty to prevent attacks from outside and crime within the state. Bearing the sword (verse 4) is more than ceremonial; it is the symbol of the authority given to the state but denied to the individual (12:19). The governing authority has the right to collect taxes, and Christians should remember Jesus' example (Matthew 17:24–27). The governing representative of the state is acting as God's servant; the Greek word in verse 4 is the one translated 'deacon' elsewhere (see pp. 192–193). In contrast to 12:7, where a deacon is an agent of God's love, here a deacon is an agent of God's justice, rewarding both good and evil. In both situations these 'deacons' are doing God's will. Christians ought to recognize this spiritual truth on which public service is founded, even though government officials may fail to recognize it themselves. On this basis we pray for those in authority over us in the hope that they will come to know Jesus Christ as Saviour and Lord (1 Timothy 2:1–4).

Its citizens' duties

Some worldly people care so little about the law that only a police force can deter them from breaking it. In contrast, Christians obey not only out of fear of being caught but also because their conscience is attuned to knowing what pleases God in the good ordering of a society (verse 5).

Tax collectors are God's servants and this is their full-time work (verse 6). This is why we pay taxes and why the Inland Revenue should be on our prayer list! Their work is to be recognized in two ways. First, we must pay taxes in order to fund the efficient running of the community at large. This does not preclude our seeking professional advice and negotiating as part of an appropriate relationship with the authorities. Secondly, tax collectors are to be given the honour and respect that servants of God deserve (verse 7). This passage might illuminate other passages of the Bible where tax collectors are mentioned, and especially Jesus' attitude to the notorious Zacchaeus (Luke 19:1–9).

Questions

1. How far can Christians or churches go in registering their objections to government injustice or wickedness?
2. How should we react when a terrorist who has killed people becomes part of the government?
3. What situations in your own society might provoke the church to say that it is more important to obey God than to obey the ruler?

Romans 13:8–14

Live as children of the light

Practical love pays its outstanding debts of money, but will never be able to settle the debt of love we owe other people. Time is running out; the return of Jesus is much nearer than we think.

Love your neighbour

Paul turns from advising us as citizens living in society to exhorting us as neighbours living in community. God wants his children to be more than good citizens who pay their taxes and obey the law of the land. In every generation a callous world desperately needs love. Because God has shared his love with us so freely, love is the debt we owe to other human beings (verse 8).

This is not the first time in Romans that Paul has used the idea of debts we owe. We have an outstanding debt to share the gospel with a needy world (1:14), to live a holy life (8:12) and to pay taxes to the state (13:7). Now we are asked to pay overdue bills and commanded to be loving people (13:8).

Love is intensely practical and is not simply a wave of emotion. It pays outstanding debts because it is unloving and unjust to put others in a precarious financial position. Paul is not forbidding loans. Jesus permits them (Matthew 5:42; 25:27). What the Bible forbids is charging high interest to borrowers and the consequent robbery of the poor by the wealthy (Exodus 22:25–27; Isaiah 3:14–15).

One debt we can never fully pay is the obligation to love, hence the phrase, 'the continuing debt to love' (verse 8). We may enjoy the peace of mind that comes from paying our bills, but we are never discharged from the debt to love, and will never be able to say we don't need to love any more. We demonstrate down-to-earth discipleship when we pay our financial bills and keep paying the love we owe (verse 9).

Breaking the commandments concerning adultery, murder, theft and coveting does great harm to people. Love, by contrast, does not harm people, but seeks to do them good and to build them up (verse 10). Believers have no natural power truly to love their neighbours. The Holy Spirit brings us the inward spiritual power to love, and, because we enjoy the most intimate union with Jesus Christ, we have the potential to reach out to a needy world with his loving words and deeds.

Live in the light

In verses 11–14 Paul reminds us as Christians of the clock and calendar of world history. Because we know what the Lord Jesus Christ has accomplished, we understand the times in which we live (verse 11). As time-watchers, Christians know it is:

Time to wake up. This is no time to be asleep. The word 'slumber' (verse 11) suggests being forgetful of all that God has done and is about to do. We must wake up because our salvation is drawing near. We know that salvation has three tenses. It is a *past* event: we have been justified (Ephesians 2:8). It is a *present* event: we are being sanctified (Romans 8:11). It is a *future* event: we shall be glorified (Philippians 3:20–21). We are living during the in-between period, when we await Christ's coming in glory, and we need to be alert to the unexpected timing of his coming. We are to live as if the day is dawning, because it is always nearer than we think.

Time to change. In the waiting period before Christ's return, we are in danger of becoming negligent. Paul uses two images to drive the point home.

First, careless Christians might get involved in the 'night-time' activities of drunken parties, sexual misdemeanours and broken relationships (verse 13). These may be appropriate for the night-time, but believers are children of the daytime. We do not yet fully live in God's daytime, but the dawn is breaking and the night is nearly over.

Secondly, we need to prepare for the day by changing our clothing. We are to put off the clothes of the night and put on the daytime clothing (verse 12), described as the 'armour of light' to symbolize the spiritual warfare in which we are engaged.

Time to be holy. Verse 14 gives us another description of the clothing we are to wear. We are to be clothed with the Lord Jesus Christ (verse 14; see also Colossians 3:12). This phrase indicates the closest possible association with Christ, and the use of his name and titles calls us to a deeper relationship with the Lord who has the right to rule every part of our lives. Do not even think about gratifying the old nature (verse 14)! We are to put on this Lord Jesus Christ as our clothing of sanctification, and thus we will be properly clothed on the glorious day of his coming.

Think what an impact Christians could make on their communities by being good citizens and loving neighbours. And all because of their love for the one who first loved them.

Questions

1. In verse 8, is Paul forbidding Christians to take out loans? Or long-term loans? Or is he just talking about defaulting on repayments? Or giving bribes? Put together 'A code of money practice for Christians'.
2. Loving one another is very hard, and yet Paul makes it a simple command to obey. How can we practise obedience to this command?
3. 'Do not think about how to gratify the desires of the sinful nature' (verse 14). How can we, perhaps unintentionally, plan to gratify such desires? What's the answer? (Note the Contemporary English Version of the earlier part of verse 14: 'Let the Lord Jesus Christ be as near to you as the clothes you wear.'

UNITY IN DIVERSITY

Romans 14:1 – 16:27

Stop and look

The practical part of the letter to the Romans commenced with chapter 12, which drew out the implications of Jesus' command to love one another.

▶ Chapter 12 had two themes. First, love is for service, so use your gifts for other people. Secondly, love must be genuine, so don't pretend.

▶ Chapter 13 continued the theme of love and tells us that love must submit, especially to the government put there by God. Love is also universal; it includes everyone without exception.

▶ Chapter 14 will teach us that love must be tolerant of other people. Paul tackles one of the most practical and challenging aspects of our Christian experience: how to enjoy fellowship with Christians whose opinions and lifestyles are very different from our own.

This problem is not new. Tensions in a fellowship and the threat of disunity have always been a danger in the life of the church. Nearly every church mentioned in the New Testament had to contend with divisions.

▶ In Corinth they were divided into groups that followed different leaders, and some members took legal action against others (1 Corinthians 6).

▶ In Galatia they were guilty of racial and cultural discrimination (Galatians 2:11–14).

▶ In Philippi a public quarrel between two women threatened the peace of the church (Philippians 4:2–3).

▶ In the house congregations at Rome, as we shall see, they disagreed over what food you could eat and which holy days you had to celebrate (Romans 14:1–2).

The Bible offers clear instructions for many moral and ethical issues, revealing God's laws for living. The Ten Commandments of Exodus 20 and the Beatitudes of Matthew 5 are prime examples of this. But sometimes the issues are less clear cut, and Romans 14 provides guidance on how Christians can relate to one another in love while differing over such issues. Our own views are not the sole standard of truth, as we often seem to think!

The heart of the disagreement is explained in verses 2–3. Paul is addressing two groups of Christians in Rome.

The first group he calls 'the strong', a group with whom he personally identifies (15:1). These are believers who fully enjoy the liberty that Christ has brought them. They have no hang-ups about which food to eat or whether to celebrate holy days. In their view every day equally belongs to God, and food is food even if it is bought from pagans. Paul affirms that God has given us freedom, but warns of the danger of despising those who have not fully entered into this Christian liberty.

The second group he terms 'the weak'. They have strict views about the Jewish food laws, the festivals and Sabbath celebrations. They consider the 'strong' group careless, indifferent and less spiritual than themselves.

This major difference of view has provoked strong words and a climate of criticism. One group now considers the other lax in spiritual things, while the other regards their fellow church members rigid and lacking liberty in the Lord. Paul suggests that in such situations we must not only be true to our principles, but also think about the effect of our actions on others.

The particular issues of food laws and festival celebrations may not be relevant to our own situation, but the value of Paul's advice lies in the permanent principles underlying it. When Christians differ today, they should

▶ identify the points of tension that threaten their church's unity, and

▶ aim to maintain the unity of the body, despite disagreeing over non-essentials.

Romans 14:1–12

Attitudes to avoid

All believers are to accept one another unreservedly in Christ. If you want a healthy church, avoid divisive attitudes.

If you have not already done so, read the 'Stop and look' section on page 208 for some helpful background to these verses.

Don't exclude the weak in faith; God has accepted them

It is easy to identify modern equivalents to the attitudes of these two groups at Rome (verses 1–3). The strong-minded are often in the majority. They regard those with a pernickety faith as stick-in-the-muds and far too traditional. They adopt that well-known attitude of group behaviour: 'As there aren't many of you, you are not worth taking seriously.'

The weak are often in the minority. They regard their strong-minded colleagues as having no scruples in matters of the faith and as taking dangerous liberties with Scripture. They may fall into contempt and spiritual pride, feeling grateful to God that at least *they* are faithful to his gospel.

When there is a dispute in the church, we must

remember that the people we disagree with are Christians. God has accepted them into his family, so who are we as family members to exclude them? However bigoted in their attitudes or ignorant of the Scriptures they may seem, we must always begin by accepting them as genuine members of the family.

Don't try to change other believers; God is at work in them

When we disagree, there is always the temptation to play the role of God in another person's life. All Christians enjoy a Master–servant relationship with the Lord (verse 4). When God is in charge of someone's life, we must not interfere.

Here it is 'the weak' who are challenged about their attitude. We need to be on guard when tempted to 'advise' people who don't share our own deep convictions. Our task is to serve the Lord, not police the saints. Peter needed a reminder of this when Jesus spoke to him about his own discipleship (John 21:21). The Lord knows far more about the spiritual development of other Christians than we ever could, and he has his ways of training them in his work. Leave things to him.

Don't base your views on what may be prejudice; seek the mind of the Lord

When we are confronted by views that conflict with our own, especially when they are held by people we respect, it is important to think the matter through with the Lord's help until we are fully convinced in our own minds (verse 5).

Note the number of times the Lord is named in verses 5–8. This reminds us that we are to form our convictions in Christ. Our minds are being renewed by the gospel (12:2), and we should use our God-given powers of reason to arrive at our own judgment as to what kind of obedience the gospel requires in a particular situation. This is not to deny the role the church community may play in offering guidance to the individual. What these verses are commanding is that we must never adopt a way of thinking or a pattern of behaviour simply because of the strong views of other people. It is the will of the Lord that is paramount.

Don't condemn other people; God will judge them

Paul uses the family term 'brother' in verse 10. Brothers and sisters with whom we strongly disagree are still fully members of God's family. The Lord alone has the right to judge the way we live, and verse 10 reminds us forcibly that each of us will have to account to the Lord for our discipleship. We often apply this verse to God's judgment of unbelievers, but in context it plainly refers to Christians who cannot resolve their differences. There are some things we can't resolve this side of heaven because our knowledge and understanding are incomplete. Paul's words in 1 Corinthians 4:5 are relevant here: 'Therefore judge nothing until the appointed time; wait till the Lord comes. He will bring to light what is hidden in darkness and will expose the motives of men's hearts. At that time each will receive his praise from God.'

Questions

1. A cohabiting couple, both newly baptized Christians and convinced that their relationship is not contrary to Scripture, want to join your church. How does Paul's teaching here affect your response to them? (You may like to study the next section before discussing this fully.)
2. What are the implications of Paul's teaching here for the 'pastoral care' of others? (Bear in mind that Paul's whole argument in Romans has been in defence of the position of the 'strong' and against the 'weak', who think they are still 'under the law'; see 7:6.)
3. If the church had really taken Romans 14 seriously, would it ever have divided into denominations?

Attitudes to cultivate

Although we enjoy freedom in Christ, we must think about the effect of our actions on others. We should cultivate attitudes that make for harmony in the life of the local church.

Our individual freedom of conscience is limited by the law of love. We must have regard to the effect our actions may have on others.

Be a good influence

None of us lives to himself or herself alone (verse 7). Our conduct influences other people. Paul follows Jesus' teaching (Mark 7:14–23) that nothing is unclean in itself (although he is applying it to food and festivals rather than to moral issues). Even so, if weaker members of the family have scruples about the food they eat and the holy days they celebrate, we must not only respect their views, but consider what *we* eat and how *we* behave on holy days.

Paul is talking (in verses 13–15) about putting a stumbling-block or obstacle in another's path. We might spiritually destroy a brother or sister if we exercise our freedom thoughtlessly and ignore the distress we cause him or her. Instead of asking, 'Will it harm me?' we should ask, 'Will it harm my brother or sister?' If the slightest danger exists, we should not do it. We must never become obstacles or stumbling-blocks to anyone for whom Christ died (verse 15).

Establish priorities

'But what about *my* freedom?' we may ask. We want to defend our liberty when it is challenged by something that seems petty. We feel we even have a *duty* to exercise our liberty of conscience in these matters. This mood is especially prevalent in the areas of money, sexuality and lifestyle. But we must guard against what we consider good being spoken of as evil (verse 16), against our liberty being interpreted as self-indulgence. The kingdom of God is more than eating or drinking; these matters are secondary. The real sign of the kingdom is righteous, peaceful and joyful lives (verse 17), not our practice regarding food and festivals. Too often the world sees only our divisions over such matters. What really pleases God are Christian communities marked by righteousness, peace and joy.

▶ *Righteousness:* because of the death and resurrection of Jesus we are loved, accepted and forgiven.

▶ *Peace:* that same love and acceptance are shared between brothers and sisters in Christ, so that we live in harmony with one another.

▶ *Joy:* a spirit of contentment arises from unclouded relationships – peace – with God and with one another.

Give up legitimate things for the sake of others

What makes for peace in a local fellowship is much more important than exercising our own liberty. The work of God must never be destroyed because of secondary issues (verse 19–20). We must always ask, 'How will this action of mine affect the peace of the church? Although I know it isn't sinful, will it cause problems for others?' We must never scandalize our brother or sister. Love must always control our liberty.

We must seek to build others up in their faith. 'Edification' (verse 19) is a rich word in Greek, that suggests building something strong. The combined ministry of the Lord and his people builds up individual believers in their faith.

Paul concludes that some things are better kept as private convictions (verse 22). It is not necessary to verbalize all our views, and we should not impose them on other members of the family.

A final warning: make sure the way you live is consistent with what you believe (verse 23).

Questions

1. Paul is talking here about putting *pressure* on brothers and sisters to act against their conscience, whether by persuasion or just by example. In Rome it was Gentile Christians pressurizing Jewish Christians to abandon the food laws. Can you think of modern examples relevant to your culture? Rewrite verse 17, inserting your examples instead of 'eating and drinking'.
2. Personal spiritual audit: why do you go to church on Sunday, or to your midweek group? Analyse your motives, and list them. Now critique your list in the light of verse 19.
3. What sort of 'fall' do you think Paul has in mind in verse 21? Some old Greek manuscripts add more words: 'fall or be tripped up or become weak'.

Romans 15:1–13

Motivation for action

When tensions threaten the peace and unity of the church, we need to support burdened Christians, follow the example of Jesus in his own ministry and gain encouragement from reading the Bible.

These verses complete Paul's teaching on how to handle diversity in the church. He has outlined attitudes to avoid and to cultivate (chapter 14), and now gives his readers examples to follow.

Support Christians with a burdened conscience

'We ... ought ... not to please ourselves' (verse 1). Those who are 'strong' are asked to be patient with whatever irritations might be created by weaker members of the family. If we find our tolerance and understanding stretched, we should measure our self-sacrifice by Christ's sacrifice.

We are called to 'bear with' our weaker friends' failings (verse 1). Paul doesn't mean 'endure' or 'put up with' people who try our patience. The Greek word means 'carry'. We help those with a tender conscience by lightening the burden they are carrying. We can do this by listening as they unburden themselves in a context of loving acceptance.

This does not mean that we should confirm people in their prejudices by meekly agreeing with their views. Lovingly challenging brothers and sisters to rethink their position on an issue, in the light of God's Word, could be a way of building them up in the faith (verse 2). The Lord always has more truth and wisdom to give us, both from his

Word and through the combined spiritual wisdom of the Christian community. Wise Christians are always open to this work of the Holy Spirit, and avoid the soul-destroying bickering that does great harm to the unity of a fellowship.

Always follow Christ's example

Paul appeals to strong Christians to tolerate the convictions of their weaker brothers and sisters because this is what Christ did (verse 3). Recalling the example of Jesus in his earthly ministry helps us greatly in our personal conflicts. Jesus did not please himself, even when people insulted him. He knew that the fierce words aimed at him were actually directed at God, since contempt for Jesus is contempt for the one who had sent him to minister (verse 3). Jesus always put the will of God before his own comfort and convenience, even when obedience meant death (Mark 14:35–36).

Jesus willingly took our place when he prayed in agony in the Garden of Gethsemane, when he was on trial before Pilate and scourged by the soldiers, and when he suffered on the cross. All this shows us how far he was prepared to go in doing the Father's will and not pleasing himself. No sacrifice we make for the sake of other people can ever make such demands on us.

During his lifetime, Christ became 'a servant of the Jews' (verse 8). Jesus submitted to Jewish customs and ceremonies, limiting his own freedom in order to heal the longstanding feud between Jews and Gentiles. God had always planned for Jesus to unite Jews and Gentiles, so that the two would become one, as Scripture reminds us (verses 9–12).

So, then, we are to accept one another just as Christ has welcomed us (verse 7). He did not wait until we were perfect before calling us his friends, but died for us while we were still his enemies (5:10). His patience with us is the pattern for our relationships with others.

Be encouraged through reading the Scriptures

The spiritual childishness of fellow-believers can severely test our patience. We need a spirit of endurance to see us through the conflicts. The Lord knows we need encouragement in the Christian life, and has given us his written Word that speaks of hope when we are tempted to despair of other believers (verse 4). When putting others before ourselves gets us down, we can read about the example of our relatives in the family of faith:

▶ Abraham yielded his rights of seniority to his nephew Lot (Genesis 13:7–9).

▶ Moses refused the privileges of the Egyptian royal family and identified with God's people when they were in slavery (Hebrews 11:24–26).

▶ Esther risked her life for the sake of God's people (Esther 4:16).

▶ John the Baptist subordinated his own work to the greater ministry of Jesus (John 3:27–30).

None of these people could be described as wimps, and all of them caught a glimpse of God's wider purpose, summarized in verse 9–12.

If we follow such examples as these, exploring the Scriptures to see how believers in earlier generations handled difficult choices, we shall support those weaker members of our family as they wrestle with their consciences on matters of faith and practice. We shall also discover something of the blessing Paul wished for his readers in prayer (verse 13).

Questions

1. The string of quotations in verses 9–12 pictures *united worship* between Jews and Gentiles as the climax of God's

whole purpose through Christ. Why should united worship be so important? What are the implications of this for relations between churches?
2. Share testimonies in your group (if possible) in response to verse 4: in what ways have you experienced the encouragement of the Scriptures?
3. 'Carry each other's burdens, and in this way you will fulfil the law of Christ' (Galatians 6:2): this verse summarizes Romans 15:1-3. List and discuss practical ways in which you could respond to this in your fellowship.

Romans 15:14-33

A missionary shares his vision for mission

Paul has a vision for taking the gospel to Spain, and needs the support of the Roman Christians in this ambitious project.

 At this point in Paul's letter we might be tempted to think he has completed his teaching and is just sharing his thoughts about his future plans and greeting his friends. But by explaining his plans for expanding his missionary work, Paul demonstrates the practical consequences of receiving Christ's righteousness.

Paul speaks of six places: Spain, Rome, Jerusalem, Corinth, Macedonia and Achaia (see the map on page 22). Paul is probably writing his letter from Corinth (Romans 16:23), where he collected an offering of money from the Christians of Macedonia and Achaia (verse 26). He plans to take it to Jerusalem, where Christians were in need (verses 25-26), and from Jerusalem he hopes to visit Rome and then

Spain (verses 24, 28). There is a familiar ring about Paul's desire to visit the congregations at Rome (1:8–15). Everything that Paul shares with them is designed to prompt their spiritual and practical support for his church-planting programme in the western Mediterranean.

He commends the congregations

The names listed in chapter 16 indicate a diverse mix of people, socially and racially. This has led to the suggestion that the church in Rome was composed of up to five household congregations. But the gospel creates fellowship, and Paul writes to this diverse community as to a competent and mature church. There were plenty of good people, well instructed in the faith and able to advise one another in Christian living (verse 14). Given the demands that Paul's letter makes on its readers, the Christians at Rome must have taken their faith seriously and thought deeply about the truths of the gospel.

He introduces his missionary strategy

Paul confirmed his calling as a servant of Christ and an apostle at the beginning of the letter (1:1), but here again emphasizes that he was called to be a missionary by the grace of God (verses 15–16). He describes his work as a minister to the Gentiles. The image of offering Gentile converts to God as a sacrifice is drawn from the closing verses of the vision of Isaiah (66:20), and reminds us that the gospel is for all nations including the inhabitants of faraway Spain. If his preaching has met success, it is because Christ has worked powerfully through Paul's words and actions (verses 17–18). The signs and wonders that accompanied his preaching (Acts 19:11–12; 28:1–10) were accomplished through the power of the Holy Spirit (verse 19). Paul is a fruitful missionary writing to a competent church.

Paul summarizes ten years' work and three missionary journeys in the phrase 'Jerusalem ... to Illyricum' (the modern day Balkans; verse 19). Within this geographical framework he has always limited his preaching to territory where no other evangelists have been, in order to lay the spiritual foundations stones of new congregations (verse 20). This church-planting ministry has been so demanding that he has been unable to visit the Christians at Rome. This same pioneering strategy is behind his missionary vision for Spain.

He requests their partnership

Paul has concluded his missionary work in the countries bordering the eastern Mediterranean and is on the verge of fulfilling a long-standing spiritual ambition to visit the capital city of the Roman Empire (verse 23) Not only is Rome a significant cultural and political centre, and the home of several congregations; the city is strategically placed as a springboard to Spain.

Paul expresses his longing to see these Christians (verse 23), confident that he and they will refresh one another spiritually (verse 32; 1:11–12).

Paul now explains the partnership he wants to develop with them. He puts a costly request to them. 'Assist me on my journey there' (verse 24) probably means assembling provisions for a long sea voyage, gathering immediate and long-term economic support and recruiting suitably gifted travelling companions from the Roman congregations.

He explains about the offering

Why is Paul making a detour from Corinth to Jerusalem on the way to his destination of Rome (verse 25)? Surely someone else from Corinth could be trusted to take the generous famine relief offering? This would have released the busy apostle to get on with his plans for the Spanish mission.

This gift of money is a sign of three Christians virtues.

First, it is *a sign of Christian compassion* (verse 25). For various reasons, including famine and persecution, the mother church at Jerusalem had been through a difficult time. In a city characterized by poverty, some of the Christians in Jerusalem may have been among the poorest of the poor. Acts 11:27–30 indicates that Paul helped to deliver offerings to this needy congregation.

Secondly, it is *a sign of Christian unity* (verse 26). The givers of the offering, congregations in Macedonia and Achaia, were mainly Gentile Christians. They would identify with the 'strong' Christians of Romans 14, who revelled in the freedom of the gospel. The believers in Jerusalem, however, would be much more conservative and line up with the views of the ' weak' believers of chapter 14. This offering crossed a racial and theological divide, and this underlines its importance. The word for 'contribution' in verse 26 is the same word often translated 'fellowship', indicating not just a generous gift of money, but a practical expression of the fellowship of the Holy Spirit, who binds together all true believers in Christ.

Thirdly, it is *a sign of a spiritual debt* (verse 27). It was God's intention that the gospel should be preached first to Jewish people (1:16). Gentile believers should feel deep gratitude at having been included in the privileges and promises given to the Jews, and should remember they are no more than a wild olive shoot grafted into the tree (11:18–20). Acts reminds us that Gentile believers first heard the good news of the gospel through courageous Jewish missionaries such as Peter and John, Paul and Barnabas, all of whom risked their lives and reputations in taking the gospel to the Gentiles. Paul has no doubt worked hard to persuade the Gentile Christians of Macedonia and Achaia of the deep symbolism of this famine offering. It is a material sign of a spiritual debt of gratitude to those who have given so much.

He invites their prayers

This is not simply Paul signing off a prayer letter with the words, 'Please pray for me.' The indications are that this was a highly dangerous mission Paul was undertaking, with no certain outcome. Later, he would be warned of the dangers that awaited him (Acts 21:10–11). He is asking the Roman congregations to pray for him in the spiritual warfare he will encounter (verse 30). He invites their prayers that he will be rescued from the opposition of unbelievers and that his service in Jerusalem will be acceptable (verse 31). In this last request there lurks a doubt. Would the conservative leadership at Jerusalem accept money from Gentile Christians? There is no record in Acts that the gift *was* accepted, although Paul's persuasion and the dire need of the poor probably meant that the gift changed hands successfully.

Paul's prayer that he would reach Rome for a time of mutual refreshing (verse 32) was eventually answered, but not in the way anyone would have expected. He had to survive trials in courtrooms and storms at sea. He nearly lost his life through a shipwreck off the coastline of Malta (Acts 27), and arrived in Rome as a prisoner. In these circumstances, Paul no doubt reminded himself of the counsel he had offered to the Roman believers: that in all things God is working for the good of those who love him (8:28).

Questions

1. Paul's collection project was a long-term, international commitment. Should the church today be doing similar things? What? Why?
2. Paul thought of himself as fulfilling Isaiah 52:15 through his ministry (the verse quoted in verse 21). How could your church imitate his adventurous strategy, in your town or region?
3. Do 'signs and miracles' have a role in preaching the gospel today (verses 18–19)? What role? Are they essential?

The house congregations in Rome

The church in Rome was probably a network of house congregations, rather than a single church meeting in one building. Church buildings were not widely in use until the fourth century and were rarely used in the third century. This is why Paul lays such emphasis on the gift of hospitality.

Some commentators identify five house congregations in chapter 16, and speculate about the kinds of members they included (based on the names and scanty information available):

▶ *The congregation of Priscilla and Aquila* (verses 3–5). A relatively wealthy home, racially mixed, and friends of Paul.

▶ *The congregation of Aristobulus* (verse 10). Upwardly mobile Jews and Greeks. Administrators by profession.

▶ *The congregation of Narcissus* (verse 11). Greek slaves with Roman sympathies, possibly unfriendly to Jews.

▶ *The congregation of Asyncritus and friends* (verse 14). Low-social-status group in a poor part of Rome.

▶ *The congregation of Philologus and friends* (verse 15). A poor underclass group with Jewish sympathies, and women included in the leadership.

If Paul had never visited Rome, how did he know so many people in these congregations? How could he greet them so personally? The answer is probably that he had met them when they had been travelling away from Rome. Priscilla and Aquila were travellers (Acts 18:1–2), and others may have moved to Rome after meeting Paul in any of the cities where he had been ministering.

We can gain a further insight into this list of names from looking back at the tensions in fellowship addressed in chapter 14. If relations between Jews and Gentiles were strained, Paul needs to demonstrate that he has fellowship with *all* the congregations in Rome. His commendations of different groups of believers may be intended to strengthen the fellowship between them.

Romans 16:1–16

Greetings to friends

These greetings underline that Romans is a real letter to real people. They are signs of the warm personal friendships that will be essential to the success of Paul's Spanish mission.

This is the longest list of names in any New Testament letter. Paul mentions twenty-six Christians, twenty-four of them by name. Over a third of those mentioned are women, which is highly unusual given the male-dominated society. The names suggest a predominantly Gentile membership with some notable and gifted Jewish personalities. While some moved in circles of influence, the majority of those mentioned are slaves, or freedmen and freedwomen, from the lower strata of Roman society.

Paul the friend

After the deep teaching of the last fifteen chapters, the list reveals that Paul is no ivory-tower theologian. The warmth and kindness in his greetings emphasize the importance of friendship. Paul had many Christian friends and he appreciated them. Look at some of the affectionate terms he uses:

▶ Epenetus, 'my dear friend' (verse 5),

▶ Ampliatus, 'whom I love in the Lord' (verse 8),

▶ Stachys, 'my dear friend' (verse 9),

▶ Persis, 'my dear friend' (verse 12), and

▶ Rufus' mother, 'who has been a mother to me' (verse 13).

The ministry of women

The list mentions nine gifted women in the church, strong evidence against the theory that Paul had a low view of women's ministry.

Phoebe (verses 1–2) was probably a wealthy woman on a business trip to Rome. She may have been the bearer of the letter to the Romans, and Paul commends her to the community in Rome, rather as we would write a reference for someone. She served as a deacon in her church fellowship in Cenchrea, the seaport for the city of Corinth, where Paul wrote Romans while based in the house of Gaius (verse 23). Phoebe was a Gentile Christian; no Jewish parents would have named their daughter after a Greek goddess.

Behind the words 'a great help' (verse 2) is the probability that Phoebe, a wealthy patron of Paul's work, had used her influence in the business community of the seaport to secure practical assistance for needy people in a hard-pressed fellowship.

Priscilla (verses 3–4) is mentioned in a number of places in the New Testament (Acts 18:2, 18, 26–28; 1 Corinthians 16:19; 2 Timothy 4:19), usually before her husband Aquila (who, like Paul, was a tentmaker). This may indicate that she was converted first; or that she had the more prominent ministry in the church; or that she was a titled lady. She and Aquila were comparatively well off and certainly given to hospitality (verse 5), and together they served as spiritual mentors to young missionaries (Acts 18:26–28). They are commended for risking their lives for Paul (verse 4). This is possibly a reference to the riot at Ephesus (Acts 19:23–40) or one of the many imprisonments that Paul experienced (2 Corinthians 11:23–27).

Junias (a male name; verse 7, NIV) is almost certainly a mistranslation for *Junia*, the wife of Andronicus (see other recent translations). Junia and her husband are not near relatives of Paul, but his 'kin', Jewish Christians, who have been in prison for their faith. They are both described as 'outstanding among the apostles' – apostles in the broader New Testament sense of travelling missionaries (1 Corinthians 12:28; 2 Corinthians 8:23; 1 Thessalonians 2:6–7). Junia and Andronicus may have been outstanding as missionaries.

Mary (verse 6), *Tryphena* and *Tryphosa* (verse 12) are all commended for their hard work in the Lord's name, as is Paul's dear friend *Persis* (verse 12). Leon Morris suggests that Paul may have intended the irony in referring to Tryphena and Tryphosa as hard workers, as their names mean 'delicate' and 'dainty'! These four women are the only Christians in the list whom Paul commends for their hard work.

Rufus' mother (verse 13) was a 'mother' to the apostle too, and one of a multitude to experience the fulfilment of Jesus' promise in Mark 3:35.

Julia and the unnamed *sister of Nereus* (verse 15) complete the list of greetings and commendations.

At the heart of this Christian fellowship in Rome is the gospel principle that women and men are equal in dignity and service, because they are one in Christ (Galatians 3:27–28).

The variety of believers

This list with its brief comments reveals a group of

Christians from a diverse background.

Some moved in circles of influence. *Aristobulus* (verse 10) may have been Herod the Great's grandson, who had ended his days in Rome. He would have been a friend of the Emperor Claudius. Aristobulus may have died, but his household still bore his name, with all the social advantages this implied.

Narcissus (verse 11) may have been the influential friend of the Emperor Claudius who was forced to commit suicide after the emperor's death. His listing here does not suggest he was necessarily a Christian himself, but members of his household were certainly believers, just as there were believers in Caesar's household (Philippians 4:22).

Rufus (verse 13) is thought to be the son of Simon of Cyrene, who carried the cross of Jesus (Mark 15:21). If this is correct, Rufus will have had a special place in the Christian community.

But there were also Christians in Rome from less influential backgrounds: *Ampliatus* (verse 8), whom Paul mentions with such affection, and *Urbanus* and *Stachys* (verse 9) all have slave names. Those in the house congregation in verse 14 have typical slave names, including *Phlegon*, a name also given to dogs. A further group of slaves, or freedmen and freedwomen, are named in verse 15.

These verses indicate that from the early days of the church, Christ gathered people from all backgrounds into his family.

Christians together in community

Paul expresses his greetings in terms of how people relate to one another in the gospel, not simply in terms of human friendship. Christian friends are described as

▶ 'in Christ' (verses 3, 7, 9, 10),

▶ 'in the Lord' (verses 8, 11, 12, 13),

▶ 'sister', 'brothers', 'mother' (verses 1, 13, 14),

▶ 'fellow-workers' (verses 3, 9), and

▶ 'saints' (verses 2, 15).

Our fellowship in the Holy Spirit can blend our cultural diversity into creative relationships.

His power also enables us to overcome those differences of temperament which so often hold us back from experiencing God's best in a Christian community. The quality of fellowship Paul was seeking for the Christians in Rome is just as much of a challenge for believers today. 'Living in community involves a daily struggle. True peace never means absence of conflict but a way of dealing with conflict' (Art Gish).

The character of service

It seems that hard work, love and courage characterized the life of the congregations in Rome.

▶ To be a Christian is to be a worker (verses 3, 6, 9, 12).

▶ To be a Christian is to be courteous and loving (verses 2, 10).

▶ To be a Christian is to be courageous (verses 4, 7, 10).

The kindliness with which Paul refers to the members demonstrates humanity. The courtesies he expresses also challenge our own relationships. We must, first and foremost, show appreciation and gratitude to those in our fellowship.

The phrase 'dear friend' (verses 5, 9, 12) speaks of those ties that bind a spiritual parent to his spiritual offspring. The holy kiss (verse 16) expresses that family relationship physically.

Questions

1. Review the ways women participate in the ministry of your church. Do they have the kind of role that Paul commends here?
2. Interestingly, Paul does not say, 'Give my greetings to …', but rather tells the Roman Christians to 'greet one another'. What does this 'greeting' actually mean? Does your church 'greet' itself like this?
3. How can we better maintain fellowship (and 'greeting') across distances, as Paul is seeking to do with this letter, and as the Roman Christians are challenged to do between their various house churches?

Romans 16:17–27

A majestic finale to the gospel symphony

Paul signs off with a pastoral warning and some greetings from friends in Corinth. He began his letter with some great themes of the gospel of God. In his closing words, he restates the same themes in a hymn of praise.

The concluding verses of the letter are like the climax of a great symphony. Paul summarizes the letter's great themes in a hymn of praise to God (verses 25–27). Before this magnificent doxology Paul gives a pastoral warning (verses 17–20) and conveys greetings from associates in his team (verses 21–24).

A pastoral warning

Following the warm greetings (verses 1–16), these verses comes a shock. There is such a change of mood that some commentators have doubted whether Paul could have written in such a style. These sentiments are in marked contrast to his diplomatic and pastorally sensitive approach to the fellowship tensions in chapters 14 – 15. But it is not too difficult to suggest some reasons for the change of mood.

▶ It is typical of Paul in his letters to declare bluntly: 'Steer clear of such people!' (See verse 17, and 1 Corinthians 16:22; Galatians 6:11–15; Philippians 3:12–21; 1 Thessalonians 2:15–16.)

▶ It is natural for Paul to open his heart following the warmth of his greetings, as though he were saying, 'I have intended telling you this at some point in the letter because it has been a burden on my heart. Now is the moment to share it with you.'

▶ It could be a postscript, responding to news recently arrived from Rome which indicates that storm-clouds of disunity are on the horizon. This is Paul saying: 'I was about to send my letter when I heard a report of the storm that is developing in the fellowship. As a matter of urgency, I advise you to keep away from people who cause divisions.'

Those who were causing divisions and constructing obstacles (verse 17) are not easy to identify. They may have been strict Jews who made life difficult for those Christians who wanted to live in the freedom of the gospel and pressurized the weak believers of chapter 14. They are known as 'Judaizers', and they appear elsewhere in the New Testament (Galatians 1:6–9). Conversely, Paul's reference to gluttony, smooth talk and deception (verse 18) may suggest Gentile libertines (see 'Antinomianism', p.

112). Paul had encountered this dangerous threat to the Christian community in 2 Corinthians 10 – 13.

Whoever they were, Paul indicates how to respond to the threat of disunity in these congregations:

▶ Identify the false teaching (verse 17).

▶ Avoid those who deceive by flattery (verse 18).

▶ Concentrate on knowing what is good, not what is evil (verse 19).

Paul urges the church members in Rome to continue in their obedience to the gospel, and to seek to grow in their powers of spiritual discernment (verse 19). He is confident that God and his people will then be victorious over Satan (verse 20). This is the first time that Satan is mentioned in this letter.

Greetings from team associates

Before Paul concludes his letter, he mentions some of his team associates who may be known to the believers in Rome, at least by name.

Timothy (verse 21) is one of Paul's most trusted colleagues and a companion to Paul on his second and third missionary journeys. He is known as Paul's son in the faith and appears in nearly all of Paul's letters. The other friends in verse 21 are not close relatives of Paul, but fellow-Jews.

Tertius (verse 22) is Paul's amanuensis, the secretary who took down Paul's thoughts and wrote the letter. What a challenging job! In line with the custom of the day, he includes his personal greeting.

Gaius (verse 23) is probably the man who was baptized by Paul (1 Corinthians 1:14) and was sufficiently wealthy to provide hospitality for Paul and for the whole church.

Erastus (verse 23) held an important post in the city of Corinth as the commissioner for public works. *Quartus* may have been his brother.

A hymn of praise to God

This is the longest of all Paul's benedictions in his New Testament letters. It restates the great themes of the whole letter, as stated in the opening verses (1:1–17). These closing verses are a song of praise from Paul's heart for all that God has revealed to him, as set down in this letter to the Roman Christians. The hymn celebrates the power of God to save people (1:16) and establish them firmly in their faith; and the proclamation of Christ (verse 25) through whom this salvation comes. God has a plan to unite Jews and Gentiles in the one body of the church. This happens through Jesus' death and resurrection and the Holy Spirit's enabling power. It is a mystery (verse 25), because we would not know God's plan unless he revealed it to us (1 Corinthians 2:6–10; Colossians 1:26). God *has* revealed his purpose (3:21). His gospel is for all the nations. God spoke his word in the Old Testament, and characters such as Abraham (chapter 4) remind us that it was always God's plan for his gospel to be international in its scope. His goal is that the nations might believe and obey his gospel (verse 26).

Glory to God! (verse 27). He is the source of all true wisdom.

In these closing verses Paul sums up God's wise plan.

▶ *We have a God who is able.* The plan of salvation unfolded in this letter is not an idle dream. By the power of the Holy Spirit it is a living reality for the church of Christ.

▶ *We have good news to share.* Jesus is Lord and Saviour for the whole world. We proclaim this gospel by word and deed, and by our lifestyle.

▶ *We have a faith to obey.* What God has revealed in his gospel is not to satisfy our curiosity but to urge our obedience.

Having made the journey through Romans with Paul and

his first-century readers, we can join with them in singing: 'To God alone be glory!'

Questions

1. Are there any modern equivalents to the people of verses 17–18, whom you must not 'greet' but 'avoid'? Think carefully and 'wisely' (verse 20), for this is an important decision.
2. If you have musical or artistic talents in your church or group, see if you can set verses 25–27 to music, or write a hymn based on it. Or put together a collage that expresses its panoramic vision of God's purposes in Christ, and its joyful praise.
3. Review your study of Romans. What have you learned? In what practical ways has God changed you and developed your discipleship? What new resolutions carry you forward from this point?

For further reading

Someone has suggested that it is possible to go through the alphabet from A to Z, and, beginning with each letter, supply the names of authors who have written on the letter to Romans. With such a galaxy of choice, from Achtemeier to Ziesler, it is an unenviable task to recommend the best books that address the wide range of crucial issues raised in the letter. However, here are some I personally have found helpful.

Commentaries

John R. W. Stott, *The Message of Romans*, The Bible Speaks Today series (IVP, 1994). Those who have heard John Stott's sermons on Romans will recognize that this is probably one of the most personally rooted of all his expositions of Scripture. There are precise explanations of all the difficult passages, and if a house-group leader is able to work with only one large commentary, this is the one to go for.

Leon Morris, *The Epistle to the Romans* (Eerdmans, 1988). This a very thorough and readable commentary. I tended to turn to Morris when studying the most difficult passages, and appreciated his balanced wisdom on crucial issues as well as the brief essays on the key themes.

C. E. B. Cranfield, *Romans – A Shorter Commentary* (T. and T. Clark, 1985). This author's major commentary on Romans was first published in 1975 and was then described as a milestone in the history of interpreting the Bible. This shorter commentary for a wider readership was written for those who have no knowledge of Greek and omits the technical footnotes and references.

Background study

James Dunn, *The Theology of Paul the Apostle* (T. and T. Clark, 1998). This deep work traverses Paul's theological thought using Romans as a road map. It is worth noting John Stott's comments on Dunn's distinctive approach to law and gospel in the opening essay in his Bible Speaks Today volume.

N. T. Wright, *Romans in a Week* (Regent College, Vancouver). This is a set of audiotapes of lectures given to Regent College students. It makes for wonderful listening in a car during a long journey. He has a lively way of communicating difficult concepts, and the tapes include the students' questions.

John Goldingay, *Evangelical Spirituality in the Light of Romans* (Grove Books, 1992). This booklet of twenty-five pages is a theological reflection on the distinct emphases of evangelical spirituality using Romans as the basic text. It offers some interesting observations on the key themes of Romans.

Reta Halteman Finger, *Paul and the Roman House Churches* (Herald Press, Ontario, 1993). A highly imaginative book designed to draw the reader of the biblical text into the socio-political context of this first-century book. She suggests it is possible to identify five house congregations in Romans 16 and that, by simulated action and reflection, twenty-first century readers can understand what it was like to be a first century believer seeking to apply the truths of the letter they had received from the apostle Paul.